D1250047

THE AGONY

OF

MODERN MUSIC

✦
✦ ✦

Henry Pleasants

SIMON AND SCHUSTER
NEW YORK

Material from *Memoirs* by Hector Berlioz, edited by
Ernest Newman, and *Giuseppe Verdi* by Francis Toye
reprinted here by permission of the publishers, Alfred A. Knopf, Inc.

Material from *Haydn, A Creative Life in Music* by Karl
Geiringer reprinted here by permission of the publishers, W. W. Norton & Company, Inc.

Material from *A Composer's World* by Paul Hindemith
reprinted here by permission of the publishers, Harvard University Press.

Material from *Selbstdarstellung* by Ernest Krenek, published by Atlantis-Verlag, reprinted here by permission of the author.

Material from *The Musical Experience* by Roger Sessions reprinted here by permission of the publishers,
Princeton University Press.

Material from Virgil Thomson's columns reprinted here
by permission of the New York *Herald Tribune*.

LIBRARY OF CONGRESS CATALOG CARD NUMBER: 54–12361
DEWEY DECIMAL CLASSIFICATION NUMBER: 780–1
MANUFACTURED IN THE UNITED STATES OF AMERICA

CONTENTS

Publisher's Note   v

Preface   vii

I. THE COMPOSER
AND HIS TIME

THE RIDDLE OF MODERN MUSIC   3

THE COMPOSER AND SOCIETY   12

THE COMPOSER AND HIS AUDIENCE   26

THE COMPOSER'S DILEMMA   37

COMPOSER AND CRITIC   47

SUCCESS AND FAILURE   62

II. THE COMPOSER
AND HIS MATERIALS

THE CRISIS OF EVOLUTION I   85

THE CRISIS OF HARMONY   97

THE CRISIS OF MELODY   111

THE CRISIS OF RHYTHM   122

THE CRISIS OF THE ORCHESTRA   137

THE CRISIS OF OPERA   152

THE CRISIS OF EVOLUTION II   166

BIBLIOGRAPHY   177

PUBLISHER'S NOTE

EVEN before its original publication in hard covers, in 1955, it was evident that *The Agony of Modern Music* was to become the most bitterly attacked and enthusiastically defended musical book of the decade. From the score or more of musicians who read it in galleys came such diverse cries as, "Scurrilous, unfair, destructive and specious" (from the Dean of the Juilliard School of Music, Mark Schubart) and "Frighteningly sound and logical" (from the eminent conductor, Erich Leinsdorf).

On publication the book became a national *cause célèbre.* It was the subject of violent debate on a number of national network radio and television programs. Professor Paul Henry Lang, who presided over the New York *Herald Tribune's* music page, devoted two Sunday two-column sermons to an emotional attack on the book and allowed its author a third Sunday's column in which to reply. The late Olin Downes, of the New York *Times,* devoted a Sunday sermon to Mr. Pleasant, mostly, but not unreservedly, endorsing his ideas. And from every city, village, hamlet and farm, it seemed, attackers and defenders sprang up.

Even the staid musicological journal of the Library of Congress, *Notes,* unbent enough to publish a satirical skit about the publication, indicating that it was an enormous best seller. Alas, Washington was sadly misinformed. For, as was internally evident from dozens of reviews and unsolicited comments, the provocative title seemed to be enough to inspire articulate passion in anyone, whether or not he had gone to the trouble of reading the balance of the text.

It is with the hope that more readers will actually grapple with the spirited but highly serious ideas presented in the book itself that the publishers are bringing it out in a low-priced format. It will now be a less shocking experience; for seven years have gone by, and much of what sounded grimly radical in 1955 has been—if not embraced as God's truth—at least acknowledged as allowable in many quarters.

PREFACE

A FEW introductory words may be in order, not to discuss what is discussed in the following chapters, but to explain what may appear superficially to be singular omissions.

There is, to begin with, no discussion of individual composers or individual compositions. Contemporary serious music is treated generically throughout. All modern music is affected more or less by the problems under discussion, and it seemed advisable to concentrate on the problems rather than dissipate the argument by a discussion of the comparative success or lack of success of various individual composers in coping with them.

Nor is there any discussion of the contemporary composer's economic problem. This is attributable neither to any lack of awareness that the composer's economic plight is unenviable, nor to any lack of sympathy. It is attributable rather to a conviction that the composer has no economic problems not directly traceable to his music. It seemed preferable, therefore, to concentrate upon the root problem.

There is, finally, no attempt to go beyond a general designation with respect to jazz. This is a book about serious or classical music, not a book about jazz. Since most popular music that is not strictly jazz is more or less influenced by jazz, it would have gone beyond the appropriate bounds of the discussion to take into account the distinction the jazzmen draw between true jazz and what they regard as its popular or commercial derivatives. What is important is not the various phases and types of jazz but its significance generically as the art music of twentieth-century society.

In short, the purpose of the discussion is to identify and stick to those basic musical and sociological factors without an appreciation of which the phenomenon of modern music cannot be understood.

I would like, however, to clarify one point raised repeatedly by hostile reviewers when this book first appeared in 1955. This is the possible inference that I equate popularity with quality. I do not. But I do believe that wide acceptance of a style or idiom is proof of its cultural vitality, regardless of its quality. There is now, within the framework of the American popular idiom, a wide range of quality, just as there always was within the European idiom. Now that the standard repertoire of orchestras, opera houses, choral societies and chamber groups is concentrated upon the surviving masterpieces, it is easy to overlook the masses of trash produced within the idiom when the idiom was still contemporary, and which enjoyed more or less passing popularity. Certainly much trash is being produced today within the American popular idiom, including a good deal of jazz, and has been produced throughout the century, but looking back on the product of fifty years, and with special regard for that which has survived, it seems equally certain that there has been much of quality, too. Generally speaking, it seems safe to observe that the most reliable criterion of quality is survival in the affection and esteem of succeeding generations—in other words, in the capacity of a given piece of music to appeal to more than the fallible fashions of a single year or a single generation. It is impossible to deny the durability of the songs of Berlin, Kern, Youmans, Gershwin, Porter, Arlen and Rodgers, or the instrumental music of Armstrong, Ellington and Basie. They have emerged from the crowd just as Bach, Haydn, Mozart, Beethoven, Brahms, Verdi and Wagner emerged from the crowd of their sometimes equally popular contemporaries. This is not to argue that American music has produced music of similar quality. Neither has modern serious music. But it is to suggest that criticism has erred in confusing objective and performance and in concentrating with persistent optimism upon composers whose objectives were congenial, regardless of the quality of their performance, while ignoring—in the face of popular acceptance—the admittedly brilliant performance of composers and musicians whose objectives fell outside the framework of aspirations associated with the exceptional accomplishments of the great composers of the European tradition.

1

THE COMPOSER
AND
HIS TIME

THE RIDDLE OF MODERN MUSIC

SERIOUS music is a dead art.

The vein which for three hundred years offered a seemingly inexhaustible yield of beautiful music has run out. What we know as modern music is the noise made by deluded speculators picking through the slagpile.

This is not to say that there will not continue to be orchestra concerts, recitals, and opera. But the time has come to recognize that Carnegie Hall, Town Hall and the Metropolitan Opera House, as well as their counterparts in other cities of the Americas and Europe, are just as surely museums as the National Gallery and the Louvre.

Nor is it to say that music is dead as a creative phenomenon. New music plays a greater part in daily life than ever before. But it has nothing to do with what is known as modern music—so-called in order to emphasize a modernity otherwise neither existent nor apparent.

The last really modern serious composer, modern in the sense that he spoke with the full authority of the cultural forces of his time, was Wagner. With him ended the long evolution of the art of music in the harmonic or European sense. All that has followed has been reaction, refinement— and desperate experimentation.

Those of his successors who have achieved genuine celebrity—Bruckner, Mahler, Strauss, Debussy, Ravel, Sibelius, Schönberg, Stravinsky, Bartok, Berg, Rachmaninoff, Prokofiev, and Shostakovich—may be described as Strauss once described himself, as triflers "who had something to say in the last chapter." They have had at least a public. For the younger men there has been none. Nothing they have written has been keyed to any considerable segment of contemporary taste or met any contemporary musical requirement other than their own ambition to be composers.

The serious composer has lost touch with the currents of popular taste. The traditional forms to which he is committed—operas, cantatas, symphonies, sonatas, and chamber music—are unrelated to modern society. They originated in and spoke for small aristocratic and bourgeois communities that had as little in common with our mass communities of today as the carriage with the jet plane or the catapult with the hydrogen bomb.

The elaboration and extension of these traditional forms to keep pace with sociological change in the nineteenth century exhausted their creative properties and destroyed their native character and physiognomy. Today they are socially and technically obsolete. To attempt to make modern use of them is like attempting to modernize a blunderbuss by adding a telescopic sight. But the composer is stuck with them. They are identified in the listener's mind with serious music —and serious music is identified with them. The composer cannot choose other materials without compromising his status as a serious composer.

It is his failure to meet contemporary requirements that distinguishes the contemporary composer from composers of any earlier epoch. Previously it could always be said that composers represented the taste and the emotional and intellectual characteristics of their own time. Haydn, Handel, Mozart, Beethoven, Chopin, Verdi, Wagner, Brahms, Strauss, and even the early Stravinsky were all popular composers. There was a demand for composers. There was a demand for their music, and they could make a living from accomodating the demand. This is not the case today. Look at the repertoire! Those compositions of this century which exercise an attractive force at the box-office, which have proven capable of survival without benefit of subsidy or subscription, can be counted on the fingers of two hands. It may be argued, of course, that all serious music requires subsidy of one kind or another. This is generally true. But evidence of popular interest, as manifested at the ticket window, is required to justify subsidies and fill subscriptions. This interest is stimulated today, not by Bartok, Berg and Stravinsky, but by Beethoven, Brahms, Wagner and Strauss.

The amount of modern music performed and recorded represents no valid challenge to the truth of this observation. Modern music is performed, recorded, and listened to, not because there is any popular demand for it, but because performers, recording companies and, to a considerable extent, serious music audiences believe that they owe the composer a hearing.

Nor should the numerous festivals of contemporary music, the grants, fellowships and commissions to contemporary composers, be interpreted as evidence of vitality. They spring from the same social assumption of an obligation to the composer. They are evidence of decrepitude, not of vitality. If modern music had any real vitality, it would take its place normally within the framework of contemporary musical life and make its own way. It would not need special promotion to obtain grudging performance and tolerant attention.

With the exception of such fleetingly attractive novelties as *Peter and the Wolf* and *Bolero,* and music straddling the border line between serious and popular, as represented more or less in the work of Gershwin, Blitzstein, Bernstein, Weill, Krenek and Menotti, all the really successful music of this century predates the First World War.

This time factor is essential to the critical comprehension of what has happened to serious music. Technical exhaustion coincided with sociological obsolescence and esthetic decay. All coincided with the ultimate agony of the nineteenth century on the battlefields of Europe in the First World War. Until then Western music had been a European affair in a European culture. Thereafter cultural leadership passed to America. Western civilization is now well into its American phase, and its music is the popular music of America.

It is natural that contemporary musicians of creative disposition and an intellectual turn of mind should seek to perpetuate the European tradition and see their names entered on the rolls of its celebrities. The great names and the great masterpieces of musical history are identified with that tradition. To abandon the tradition would be to abandon the implications of superior cultural values associated with it.

One of the singularities of a Western civilization no longer European is the habit of its intellectuals to think of culture in European terms, as though culture were somehow exclusively synonymous with European accomplishments and tastes in music, painting, sculpture, architecture, and literature.

Thus the European composer, rebelling against the cultural Americanization of Europe, writes as if the evolution of European music were divinely ordained to be infinite. The American composer, seeking to continue the European tradition at home, flatters himself that he may be able to enrich it with new vitality drawn from his own new cultural environment.

This is a false refuge for a type of reaction that has little to offer but wishful thinking expressed in academic stylistic experimentation.

Among those who recognize the truth of this are the composers. It should not be surprising. They are, after all, in a better position than others to recognize the exhaustion of the resources with which they work, and the lack of popular interest in their efforts. Notable among them was the late Arthur Honegger who, in his little book, *Je suis compositeur*,[1] wrote:

"The collapse of music is obvious. . . . Nor is anything to be gained from resisting it. . . . The profession of composer discloses the singularity . . . of a person who troubles himself to produce something for which there are no consumers. . . . The contemporary composer is a gate-crasher trying to push his way into a company to which he has not been invited." *

This penetrates to the essence of the matter. The familiar spectacle of the contemporary work sandwiched between Beethoven and Brahms exposes the gate-crasher in full silhouette, sneaking into the concert hall under the coattails of the elect. It also shows the conductor's part in the conspiracy. There is Beethoven on one side to make sure that the audience comes in. There is Brahms on the other side to make sure that it does not get out until the gate-crasher has been heard.

Few people like modern music much. Even fewer like much of it. Most people do not like it at all. But it continues to be written, played, and talked about as if it mattered. Why? Who cares?

* *Je suis compositeur*, by Arthur Honegger. Copyright by Editions du Conquistador, Paris, 1951.

Well, the composers care, of course. It represents their bid for status and fame, if hardly any longer for money. And the conductors care. It breaks the tedium of the standard repertoire. It may bring a certain useful notoriety, and it will certainly bring credit for enlightened courage. The critics care, too. It relieves them of tiresome critical cud-chewing about the familiar performance of familiar pieces. Some in the audience care, for it reassures them on the continuity of their musical culture.

Thus the answer would seem to be that the contemporary composer, while he fulfills no contemporary musical requirement, may fulfill a social one—or at least the requirement of a certain segment of society. He is not, in other words, alone in his delusion that he is perpetuating the European tradition, nor in the conviction that it must, somehow, be perpetuated. As long as he is there, bad as he may be, all is not over.

This is hardly the point of view, however, of the majority of musical laymen who go to the opera house to hear Verdi, Wagner, and Puccini, and to the concert hall to hear Beethoven, Brahms, Tchaikovsky and Strauss. Their toleration of the gate-crasher reflects only a well-mannered reluctance to make a scene or a want of confidence in their appraisal of him as an intruder and impostor. This combination of good manners and timidity is enthusiastically encouraged by the gate-crashers and their sponsors.

In former times contemporary music survived despite opposition from critics and professional musicians because the public liked it. Today it languishes despite critical and professional support because the public will have none of it. That it survives at all, or at least continues to be played, is due simply to the fact that the public no longer has anything to say about it.

Audience taste still determines the selection of the standard repertoire; for it is the standard repertoire that sustains the expensive institutions identified with serious music. Here the public cannot be ignored. Modern music cannot sustain anything, and the public can be ignored with impunity in its selection, particularly since the appeal of the standard repertoire is still so strong that the public may be counted upon despite the novelties.

In modern music popular success has ceased to be a criterion. All that counts is the opinion of the professionals—conductors, composers, and critics—none of whom gives a damn what the public thinks.

Under normal competitive circumstances this sort of exclusive expert sponsorship would not suffice to effect the survival of so unpopular a phenomenon as modern music. In other fields today, in the theater, moving pictures, radio, television, literature, and architecture, survival is impossible without popular interest and approval. Only in painting and sculpture is professional opinion accorded a similar monopoly.

Only in painting and sculpture does so bad a product get so much flattering professional attention. And only in painting and sculpture is such a state of affairs accepted so placidly as proper. Not only have the professionals taken over, lock, stock and barrel; they have even persuaded the public that this is the way it should be!

All the conventions of our musical thinking are calculated to convince the layman that tolerance is the finest of all virtues. For him who finds tolerance difficult, there is the spectre of a future generation's rapture, the implied suggestion that to voice his derogatory opinions is to risk going down in history as an ass.

The layman is taught that the history of music is a record

of continuous progress and sturdy enlightened development, accomplished by farsighted, courageous, and dedicated men in the face of horrendous obstacles put in their way by benighted, small-minded, and malicious professional and lay Philistines.

Among the bromides of his education is the legend that musical masterpieces are never appreciated in their own time. This is the composer's trump in any argument about modern music. Its general acceptance offers the only completely satisfactory explanation of why modern music is tolerated. That this should be so is the most fascinating mystery of our musical life; for the history of music is an accumulation of evidence of the legend's fraudulence.

In short, the layman is encouraged to like everything, to appreciate things for what they are, and not to find fault because they are not something else. He is admonished not to make critical comparisons. A catholic taste, he is told, is synonymous with cultural enlightenment. Forgotten is Oscar Wilde's excellent injunction that to like equally and impartially all schools of art is to betray the soul of an auctioneer. Small wonder, then, that the layman is an inhibited and confused critic!

But of such is the folklore of music appreciation, that compendium of what Hindemith has so rightly called "noncommittal aestheticism, popularization, and sugar-coated banality."[2] It is the fashion of our musical community to accept it as the indisputably correct interpretation of musical history, and to make it the basis of critical dogma. It is the most significant factor of our musical life.

It permits the composer to go on writing as if music were not intended to be heard and enjoyed by ordinary mortals— and still be played!

It permits the conductor to select from this production according to his own convenience, as if convinced that his audiences are morons—and be re-engaged!

It leaves the audiences docile and polite, accepting this abuse as if determined to prove their disparagers correct—and coming back for more!

It is a very curious situation.

THE COMPOSER AND SOCIETY

THIS curious situation is unfathomable without taking into consideration society's curious conception of serious music.

The key would seem to be the word "understanding." No other word is used so often in the discussion of music. Certainly no other is used with less precision. The examples are obvious: "I love music but I don't understand it." "I can't say that I liked the new symphony, but then, of course, I don't understand modern music." "It was interesting. I might like it if I could ever learn to understand it." And so on. Everyone has heard such statements, and most people have uttered them.

The notion that music is something that has to be understood persists despite the fact that no one has ever defined precisely what it is that one is supposed to understand. It is possible, of course, to understand compositional structure, the elements of melody, harmony, and rhythm that go into it, and the techniques by which structure is achieved. But this is not what is meant by understanding.

The implication is rather of indefinable meaning than of definable structure. Music is assumed to convey to the initiated an intelligible communication, preferably of philosophical character. The language of criticism and commentary abounds in such terms as depth, struggle, conflict, suffering, solitude, confession, obscurity, enigma, reflection, introspection, imagination, lucidity, fantasy, mystery, idea, ideology, sentiment, communion, description, expression, spirituality, dream, poet, etc.

This terminology derives from the subjective character of the great representative music of the nineteenth century. This is music of the era loosely described as romantic. It is the music that comprises by far the greater part of the standard repertoire of our symphony orchestras and opera houses. It is the music for which the great majority of serious music lovers have an uninhibited preference, and it is the music to which they refer when they speak of serious, or, even more loosely, classical music.

Insofar as the layman understands this music, or thinks that he understands it, he does so in terms of the philosophical, psychological, mystical, and biographical interpretation that is the substance of such professional criticism, appreciation, and commentary as comes his way. The interpretation of the opening measures of Beethoven's Fifth Symphony as representing fate knocking at the door is a serviceable example.

Such discussion is not and cannot be precise. No two critics or commentators agree completely on the substantive meaning of any given piece. Often enough, two analyses, even by two composers, may yield diametrically opposed conclusions. Thus the layman is confronted with a mystery.

He may be aware that the mystery is insoluble even to the professionals. But he modestly assumes that they are closer to enlightenment than he, and thus honors them with the respect due the initiated. Among the latter the composer, being closest to the mystery, the chosen instrument for the propagation of its enigmas, emerges as a sort of high priest, a man supernaturally ordained to communicate with the Infinite.

Thus it is that society tends to think of the composer as a hallowed member of the community, a person of such extraordinary endowment and calling as to entitle him to extraordinary indulgences. Among these is the privilege of reversing the usual relationship of individual and society.

Normally, a man's position in society is determined by what he is reckoned to have done for it, as reflected in pleasure or such other benefits as society may feel it has derived from his labor. The composer's position is determined by what he is reckoned to be doing, not for society directly, but for his art. It is assumed that if he serves his art well, society will benefit eventually. Society's cultural position, in turn, is determined by what it is reckoned to be doing for the composer. In short, since there is now little immediate enthusiasm for what the composer does, he is assumed to be exempt from the law of supply and demand.

Society's obligation to the composer is recognized wherever Western music is widely accepted and played. The composer is regarded as a source of spiritual and cultural enrichment and, as such, deserving of the encouragement and support of the less sublimely endowed. He is also assumed to know better than society what is culturally good for it. He is, thus, not only permitted, but even encouraged to write his own ticket.

This assumed obligation is honored in various ways in various parts of the world. In Europe, the Soviet Union, South and Central America, and to some extent in the United Kingdom and the Commonwealth, it is accepted as a government charge. In the United States it is left to the musical community, to be discharged through paid attendance, conscientious, open-minded attention, and philanthropy.

Recognition of the composer as standing above and beyond the law of supply and demand is common to all systems. Totalitarian systems hedge their generosity with the requirement that the composer serve totalitarian society by writing the kind of music totalitarian governments deem suited to their plans for shaping the society they govern. But even thus restricted, the composer is expected to act as the medium of musical inspiration. Totalitarian governments are not different from free society in their estimate of the serious composer as a social ornament.

The result in any case is to separate the composer from society. In free societies he is assumed to be responsible only to his Art, as interpreted by what he calls his own artistic integrity. In totalitarian societies his special calling is recognized. He is simply held responsible to his government for the manner in which he responds to it. In neither case does a popular estimate of his value, as evidenced by popular enthusiasm for his product, carry any weight.

This concept of the composer as the servant of a vague identity known as Art has encouraged society to take for granted the present widening gulf between new serious music and the community of serious music lovers. The result is disaster. It separates artistic evolution from social evolution. But it is universally applauded by a society that fails to remember, or has never understood, that artistic evolution unrelated to social evolution is unlikely to be evolution at all.

The masterpieces of the standard repertoire date from periods when the relationship of artist and society was the reverse of what it is today. In the seventeenth, eighteenth, and even the nineteenth centuries gifted composers were numerous. Their purpose was to please, and to prosper from approval. The musical art took its place among other crafts and professions, and society was not so much disposed to confuse musical invention with revelation.

Bach, Handel, Mozart, and even Beethoven all worked at composition for a living. They were expected to give their employers and benefactors what the latter wanted. They did, and without compromise. They wrote the kind of music that was fashionable in the society whose tastes and habits shaped the cultural profile of the time. They wrote because there was a demand for their product, and distinguished themselves by writing better than their contemporaries.

The same was true under somewhat different circumstances of many later composers. Rossini, Donizetti, Bellini, Meyerbeer, Weber, Verdi, and Puccini all made a handsome living from composing operas. Even Wagner never suffered from lack of popularity. His difficulties were in getting his works produced, not in getting them liked.

Among the non-opera composers, Schubert, Mendelssohn, Schumann, Chopin, Liszt, and Brahms all derived a sizable proportion of their income from commissioned compositions and the sale of their published works. What they earned additionally as teachers, players, and conductors was directly related to the fame and popularity derived from their compositions. The same holds true right down to our own time in the circumstances of such popular composers as Strauss, Ravel, and Stravinsky.

In other words, our view of the composer as independent of the law of supply and demand, as a sort of autonomous satellite of society, is of very recent origin. Previously the composer was regarded as a working professional. His prosperity was determined, as in other walks of life, by what society, uninhibited in its judgment, thought of his work. Now, as the successor of a long line of composers whose accomplishments were extraordinary, he is accorded an extraordinary position.

We are thus faced with the paradox of contemporary society deferring to composers not worth the deference in an effort to make up for the assumed former failure of society to defer to composers who were. In attempting to correct the alleged previous mistake of under-evaluating the greatly gifted, contemporary society compounds the error by over-evaluating composers who have yet to demonstrate that they are gifted at all.

This is attributable, at least in part, to the fact that the accomplishments of the older composers were so extraordinary as to cast a reflected glory upon the whole profession of musical composition, a glory so concentrated and so magnified by critical attention and admiration that society is still blinded by it.

It is not, however, a matter of excellence alone. The music of the seventeenth and eighteenth centuries offers examples of composers whose sheer musical invention surpassed both in quality and facility that of the nineteenth century masters without persuading the society for which their music was produced that it was confronted by a mystery.

Our own view is a distillation of the nineteenth century tendency to think of music in philosophical terms and of the composer as a demi-divinity called to translate to lesser mortals his glimpses of enlightenment. Hence the habit of thinking of music as something in which understanding is thought to be superior to enjoyment, or at least essential to the experience of a superior pleasure. Since music itself offers no tangible clues to this understanding, society has looked for understanding in the tangible materials of its composers' lives.

The nineteenth century was an age of self-conscious introspection, an age in which eccentricity appeared, not as a neurotic affliction, but as evidence of superiority to the social average, as a symbol of enlightened individualism. The century pictured itself in terms of the individual silhouetted against the background of society. Formerly one had thought of the individual as an integral part of society and as a reflection of it. Now society thought of itself as a composite of individuals, and of its artists as champions of individualism. Not the social sobriety of Bach, Handel, and Haydn, but the social intransigence of Wagner, Berlioz, and Liszt was its model.

Under the circumstances it was natural that the music of the time should have had a subjective character, and that music of subjective inspiration should have proved so popular. The best of its composers were not only introspectively disposed, both personally and nationally; they also thought of composition as a musical sublimation of subjective philosophical contemplation and speculation.

It was inevitable that a society thus preoccupied with man's struggle with his nature and his environment should have found a special fascination in the work of those whose social equilibrium was most dramatically disturbed and for whom the struggle was most intense. Thus the extraordinary percentage of maladjusted men among the great composer names of the century.

Let them pass for a moment in review: Beethoven, Schubert, Schumann, Berlioz, Chopin, Liszt, Wagner, Brahms, Franck, Tchaikovsky, Moussorgsky, Smetana, Dvorak, Wolf, Bruckner, Mahler, etc. They are an odd lot, everyone of them more or less drastically at odds with himself and with society, in several cases to an extent which led to medically confirmed insanity.

History has treated their infirmities with sympathy and indulgence, and with a good deal of sentimentality. The standard biographies are devoted to a study of how their troubles, their introspective preoccupations and self-questionings, their impatience with society and society's occasional impatience with them, found expression in their music.

It is suggested that there is something superficial about the man at peace with himself and society, and something inferior about music which has no other purpose than to please. It is rather more than implied that some sort of maladjustment is a prerequisite for creative greatness, and that such self-expression is music's noblest purpose; in short, that the sensitiveness which makes the world too much for the individual seeks, and in the gifted finds, an escape route to the Infinite.

At the same time, society is blamed for its composers' troubles. Much is made, for instance, of Schubert's poverty, and Vienna has suffered abuse for its alleged neglect of the most gifted of its native sons. It is unthinkable to suggest that Schubert did next to nothing to call attention to himself in a competitive world. It is even worse to suggest that he might have done very well had it not been for a pathological aversion to working for a living—or had he even been circumspect in spending what he earned from his hobby. This was, by the standards of the times, considerable.

There is a droll inconsistency here. Assuming, as many biographers seem to do, that unhappiness and social conflict are essential to great creation, then Vienna could not have sponsored Schubert without disturbing precisely those circumstances which are thought to have contributed most importantly to his finest music.

This inconsistency runs like a thread through musical history from Beethoven's time on. The composer is represented as in conflict with society, as a person of such superior sensibility that society is too much for him—and he too much for society. His greatest music is seen as a product of this conflict, and its survival as a symbol of the composer's victory. Society, in turn, is pilloried for having presented the obstacles without which greatness is assumed to be impossible.

A still more striking inconsistency, and one little emphasized by history, is the fact that all these composers were immensely successful. Out of the conflict between composer and society came a product as pleasing to society as to the com-

poser. Musical history and its readers, with a common pen-
chant for the sentimental and the dramatic, over-emphasize
the failure of society to offer instantaneous recognition and
underplay the composers' subsequent successes and celebrity.
They also distort the factor of opposition, presenting it, not
as a kind of recognition, but as a form of social sin.

Would it not be more sensible to admit that recognition
comes slowly to most in this imperfect and self-centered
world, and that normally it is not accorded immediately and
unanimously on the basis of a single accomplishment, but
rather on the basis of a long record of accomplishment sustained and surpassed? Would it not also be well to admit
that controversy and opposition, failing a utopian universal
unanimity, are as eloquent forms of recognition as this world
can bestow?

Certainly! But this would destroy the popular image of
the composer as a person of exceptional endowment condemned to suffer exceptional adversity for the ultimate exceptional benefit of society. A pertinent example of this
image is provided by the English critic and historian, W. H.
Hadow, in his appreciation of Beethoven and the *Missa
Solemnis:* [3]

"We have a vivid picture of him, wild, haggard, dishev-
elled, oblivious of sleep and food, tearing the music from
the very depths of his being, and bending it by sheer force
into the appointed shape . . . The whole character of the
Mass is in keeping with the circumstances of its production.
It is gigantic, elemental, Mount Athos hewn into a monu-
ment, scored at the base with fissure and landslip, rising
through cloud and tempest, beyond the reach of human gaze.
It has been called dramatic, but the word is ludicrously in-
adequate; if this be drama, it is of the wars of gods and
giants, with lightning for sword and the clamorous wind for
battle cry . . . We are brought face to face with that ulti-

mate Reality of which beauty itself is but a mode and an adumbration."

This is also a good example of the kind of fanciful criticism that has encouraged the lay listener to believe in the distorted image of the professional composer which so complicates his enjoyment of the masterpieces and so inhibits his judgment of modern music.

It matters little that the less impressionable may find less labored creation than Beethoven's to be evidence of greater genius. Hadow himself compares Beethoven with Mozart, the latter with "the tunes coming to him as he rode in his carriage; the fugue composed while he was copying out a prelude; the overture written impromptu in a single night. It is a far cry to those months of concentrated effort and the prize wrested from fate by such titanic energy and self-will." There is no question but that historians and their readers have recognized the greater effort as superior, or at least more exciting, and have preferred what Paul Henry Lang has so aptly called Beethoven's "fling at the Universe" [4] to Mozart's sovereign mastery.

"The way from Polycletus to Lysippus," says Spengler,[5] "and from Lysippus to the sculptors of the Groups of the Gauls is paralleled by the way from Bach by Beethoven to Wagner. The earlier artists felt themselves masters of the great form, the later artists its slaves. While even Praxiteles and Haydn were able to speak freely and gaily within the limits of the strictest canon, Lysippus and Beethoven could only produce by straining their voices."

The contemporary composer, if not the contemporary critic, may agree with this, but the fact remains that for a hundred and fifty years musical history has been made, not by men who could "speak freely and gaily within the limits of the strictest canon," but by men for whom such limits, far from being a stimulating challenge, were an abhorrence.

It has been the past critical fashion to treat this abhorrence as an enlightened rebellion against the artificial constraints of the prescribed forms. By a singular sort of partisan
rationalization history has turned the tables in a manner il-
lustrated by Henry T. Finck when he wrote of Chopin: "We
are asked to believe that Chopin . . . could not write a correct sonata. Chopin not able to master the sonata form? The
fact is that the sonata form could not master him!" [6]

Such is the romantic view. Society applauds it. It is not
applauded, however, by the contemporary composer. He
realizes better than anyone else what the formal licenses of
his predecessors have cost him in exhausted materials, and
he would like nothing better than to get back to a more
orderly type of music. This nostalgia is common to the profession both in Europe and America, and it accounts for the
overwhelmingly neo-classical flavor of most modern music.
It is one of the points where the contemporary composer and
his audience find themselves hopelessly at odds. For the lay
listener is not afflicted with it.

The nineteenth century composer had a nostalgia, too. But
it was for emancipation, not for discipline. Preoccupied with
his own identity, and pompously documenting its importance
in autobiographical composition, he nevertheless produced
music in which his listeners not only found pleasure but also
found their own preoccupations sublimely reflected.

The contemporary composer, preoccupied, not with himself nor with society, but with the problem of how to continue in a tradition esthetically and technically exhausted,
and contemptuous of the music that exhausted it, produces
a music of technical excogitation in which the listener finds
neither pleasure nor the reflection of anything of the least
concern to him.

The contemporary composer is the most ambivalent of
creatures. He likes to think of himself as an ordinary fellow,

unblemished by the personal eccentricities and esthetic pretensions of his predecessors, as a man who dresses normally, wears his hair at a normal length and speaks in a down-to-earth vernacular. But he covets the applause of an audience that still likes to think of the composer as standing somewhere between the temporal and the eternal, as its interlocutor with infinity.

He carries this social conformity over into his music, at least to the extent of writing what he likes to consider down-to-earth music, free of philosophical and psychological hidden inner meanings. He abjures interpretive program notes. He believes that his music should speak for itself, and is confident that it has something to say. Aaron Copland summed this attitude up well in his remarks about "Les Six" in his early book, *Our New Music*: [7]

"Les Six symbolized a new twentieth century type of composer. They ended forever (we hope) the nineteenth century conception of composers as long-haired geniuses who live and starve in garrets. To Les Six the creative musician was no longer the high priest of art but a regular fellow who liked to go to night clubs like everybody else. What they wanted to write was 'une musique de tous les jours,'—a more everyday kind of music. Not the kind you listen to with your head in your hands, lost in revery or some sort of emotional fog. All that was ended. We were to listen now with eyes open to music that was 'down to earth' as Hollywood would say."

What they forgot—and what Copland forgot—is that the serious music audience is not a down-to-earth audience but one that still prefers the personal and mystical glamor of a kind of music it doesn't fully understand and which the contemporary composer understands to the point of finding it a bit ridiculous.

The real down-to-earth audience, the popular music audience, on the other hand, is amply supplied with a down-to-earth music of its own which the serious composer, by definition, cannot write, and with which his own product cannot compete, if only because its down-to-earthiness has an intellectual cast neither charming nor intelligible to the popular audience.

In short, the composer would like to please, but is not pleased to write what pleases society, or at least that part of society which comprises his audience. Society would like to please the composer, whom it regards as an ornament and as a comforting guarantee of cultural continuity, but it is not pleased by what he writes. The situation is tolerated only because both composer and society have been persuaded to believe that this is the way it has always been.

Society's concept of the composer-audience relationship is as distorted as the composer's. It imagines the present situation to be a replica of what has been happening for generation after generation for a century and a half—which it isn't—and assumes that the next generation will be listening to this music with rapture—which it won't.

The essence of all this is that both composer and audience regard their relationship in terms which have neither artistic nor social validity and which, in most respects, never had. It is not a satisfactory relationship, but the habit of reading bromides rather than history, and the bromidic character of much that passes for history, have left both parties with neither the inclination nor the vigor to do anything about it.

It is like an unhappy marriage which has lasted for a long time and to which both partners have grown accustomed. It is not ideal, but it is tolerable, and seems to enjoy social approval. It offers stability of a kind, if not much pleasure, and the association is by now so much an accepted pattern that the thought of change is more frightening than the reality of continuity.

In a way, however, it goes farther than that. The composer is the smarter of the partners, and the better informed. Society may think that this is all there is to it, all that may be expected of it—and resign itself to enduring what it assumes will be the next generation's pleasures. The composer may give lip service to this view, and encourage it, in order to reassure both himself and his audience. But down deep in his heart he knows better.

He knows that the present relationship of composer and audience is not what it used to be or what it ought to be now. He knows that there is something wrong. And in his moments of most lucid thinking he asks himself why?

THE COMPOSER AND HIS AUDIENCE

IT RARELY occurs to the contemporary composer that the blame for his estrangement from the serious music audience might lie with himself.

He finds it difficult to admit that he is simply not producing anything that provokes a sympathetic response in his listeners. He forgets that it is the purpose of music to provoke such a response, and that all superior music in the past has provoked it.

Instead, he blames the audience. He accuses it of lazy indulgence in the familiar, of unwillingness to make the effort required to "understand" him. He refuses to believe that the audience prefers the familiar only because it is still the best that can be had. He will not face the hard fact that if he wishes to win the audience he must compete with the familiar—and on the audience's terms.

He cannot accept this challenge. It would mean competition with music he knows is better than his own. It would also require his acknowledgment that understanding is a two-sided affair, that he should make as great an effort to understand his audience as he expects the audience to make to understand him.

This would imply equal rights for composer and audience in the determination of musical evolution. The composer does not believe in them. To allow himself to be governed in the slightest degree by his audience's tastes would be to compromise his sacred artistic autonomy. Roger Sessions, in his *The Musical Experience*,[8] presents the composer's point of view in the following characteristic fashion:

"What does the listener demand from music? The answer will inevitably be that a variety of listeners want a variety of things. But on any level it may be taken for granted that the listener wants vital experience, whether of a deeply stirring, brilliantly stimulating, or simply entertaining type.

"If we understand this we should understand, too, that the composer can effectively furnish it only on his own terms. He can persuade others to love only what he loves himself, and convince only by means of what fully convinces him. It is for this reason that the artist must be completely free, that such a question as I have just stated here can ultimately have no importance to him."

This is as much as to say that if composer and listener, each pursuing his own way, should happen to arrive at a common objective, all would be well and good. But it would require a coincidence by which the listener happened to choose a way and an objective identical with the composer's. The latter may not move an inch from the path marked out for him by what he is pleased to call his integrity. To think of adjusting his course to meet the tastes of his listening partner is ruled out as that most hateful of words in the composer's vocabulary: compromise.

A fitting parallel would be an automobile industry that produced automobiles without regard for the tastes and requirements of the buyer. Obviously, this would be bad for business. But it is blasphemy to speak of music as business, or of the listener as a consumer, despite the fact that most great music has been written on that basis. Hence the confident arrogance of the statement that for the composer the

question of what the listener wants from music "can ultimately have no importance to him."

Elsewhere in this book Mr. Sessions states: "Without this
complete freedom for the artist to create according to his
impulses there can be no development. Music, or any art,
can in such a case only follow the law of the lowest common
denominator; in providing the public with 'what it wants' it
will inexorably tend to provide it with what is understood
with least effort."

In other words, evolution is possible in the sense of development only when society follows the composer. For the
composer to reflect society by reacting to its tastes would be
to strangle development. The public is lazy, and its taste is
bad; if left to its own devices society must go straight to the
cultural dogs!

Such is the composer's estimate of the audience. He holds
out to it the hope of salvation only if it will follow him. He
goes his own way in any case, composing because he must
and as he must. The cultural fate of the audience is up to
the audience. If it chooses the path of least resistance—well,
to hell with it!

Aaron Copland has carried this attitude a step further.
What the audience wants is, to him, not only of no importance; it is also of no interest. Thus, in one of his recent
books, *Music and Imagination*,[9] he can write without em-
barrassment:

"Parenthetically I should like to call attention to a curious
bit of artist psychology. The thought that my music might
or might not give pleasure to a considerable number of
music lovers has never particularly stirred me."

The full implications of this can best be understood by
contrasting it with the letter Haydn wrote to the musical
community of Bergen on the Baltic Sea island of Rügen in

response to a letter thanking him for *The Creation*, which they had just performed there for the first time:

"You give me the pleasant conviction . . . that I am often the enviable source from which you and so many families susceptible of true feeling derive pleasure and enjoyment in domestic life. What happiness does this thought cause me! Often, when contending with obstacles of every sort . . . a secret feeling within me whispered: 'There are but few contented and happy men here below; everywhere grief and care prevail; perhaps your labors may one day be the source from which the weary and worn, or the man burdened with affairs may derive a few moments' rest and refreshment.' What a powerful motive for pressing onward!" [10]

The implications are plain. In Haydn's day composers wrote to please their listeners, and were delighted and even moved when their listeners were pleased. Their point of departure was a style and a compositional frame of reference with which their listeners were familiar. This did not rule out novelty and originality.

Haydn himself delighted in giving his listeners a surprise, even a shock now and then. But he reckoned in terms of what they were accustomed to hear and what they were known to enjoy. He had both more sense and more humility than to burden them with more novelty than he estimated they could assimilate. Nor would it have occurred to him to think of this as a disgraceful compromise.

No one has exposed the character of the contemporary composer's relationship to his audience more vividly than one of the most famous of their number, Paul Hindemith. In his *A Composer's World* [2] he lets his colleagues have it with both barrels:

"Finally, never forget to assert your modernity. The proclamation of one's modernity is the most efficient cover for a bad technique, unclear formulations, and the lack of a personality. Not only that! Writing what is called modern music lifts you automatically into a world-wide society of composers with similar tendencies. The inevitable overweight of inefficiency in such a society must sooner or later tend toward the protection of the feeble composer and to an escape from the brutal selection of quality in the normal course of musical life.

"Thus a solitary, esoteric style will be the result, the well-known secret language understandable only to the initiated, removed from any musical desires of an ordinary music lover, and thriving under hothouse conditions. No wonder, then, that clashes occur whenever a piece of this kind appears in our commonplace concert life . . . The so-called modernist composer and the ordinary concert-goer, each following his own line of interest and totally disregarding the other's considerations, are drifting apart, and the gap between them is widening with each further performance of an obscure piece.

"If you want to follow the practice of most of your colleagues, you will not ask what are the facts that caused this deplorable situation. Never will it occur to you that the composer may be guilty, that the consumers are not the only ones to be blamed. You rather accept the situation as an unalterable fact, grown out of historical necessity; as an unfavorable condition into which we are born. On this basis you will not cease to make your complaints heard: The neglect of our modern music is a burning disgrace; we shall not become the martyrs of the general conspiracy against our works!

"And then you meet with your fellow sufferers in international, national, and local societies for contemporary music; you arrange festivals, symposia, and anything else for the propaganda of your products and those of your fellow high-brows. In short, the entire machinery of promotion is starting its noisy gyration."

To which both the composer-colleague and the layman may well cry: "Bravo, bravo; but look who's talking!" It was a fellow composer, Constant Lambert, who described Hindemith's music as "busy and colorless, without any distinguishing spiritual or national quality. . . . Here at last is the musical equivalent of the robot and the adding machine." [11]

It is not that the contemporary composer does not know his audience. As Copland has said, "There is no disagreement as to what audiences want; they want what they already know, or something that sounds like it." [12] But now, unlike the situation in Haydn's time, there is a difference of taste between composer and public. What pleases the public does not please the composer. Finding little sympathy from his audience, the composer turns to his colleagues for comfort, forming a society of musical snobs. From this forum he and his fellows present a united front to the non-professional musical world and claim for themselves the right to decide what is music and what is not.

The most articulate spokesman of this society in the United States has been Virgil Thomson. Nowhere has the professional attitude toward the lay audience been so frankly stated as in his column in the *Herald Tribune* of Sunday, February 14, 1954:

"Critics, composers, and performing artists have in common the advancement of music. They are also busy advancing their own careers, and any workman in the arts is entitled to consider his own career important. Every career is, as a matter of fact, because the music of this our time is the music composed by the present writer and his colleagues, nothing else. And this goes for music criticism in our time too. All living musicians—and no critic is respected by his readers unless he is a musician, has some skill in the technique of music and some responsibility to it as an art—all living musicians, I say, are part of one great band (or conspiracy, if you will) vowed to the defense of the musical faith and to its propagation.

"Their methods of going about this differ widely, and they are always treading on one another's toes. Treading on the toes of composers and performers is, indeed, considered by many layman as the main business of critics. This is not so. Their main business, really their only business . . . is explaining the creative or executant artist to the public. Explaining the public to the artist is management's business and that of older artists. Defending the public against the artist is nobody's business, not the impresario's, nor the politician's, nor the clergy's, still less than that of the critic, whose living depends on the survival of the art he speaks for."

There you have it! The professionals banded against the non-professionals, the critic admitted to the fraternity on the assumption that he is also a musician of sorts, and as such even granted the privilege of an opinion, although advised that he should keep it to himself if it is derogatory, since to do otherwise would be to betray the brotherhood!

Yet for all this united front, for all the "noisy gyration of the machinery of promotion," the composer fails to win his audience. One may argue that for a profession making such a show of indifference to audience reaction this should be neither surprising nor disturbing. But the composer has his share of vanity, and for all his big talk he craves approval.

That he does not get it is attributable neither to the laziness of the audience, nor to the refusal of the performer to stuff modern music down his audience's throats. Actually audiences are more patient than they should be, and performers play more modern music than can be justified by the quality of the music or the wishes of their audiences.

It is attributable to what he composes. Here again we are indebted to Virgil Thomson. Take for example the following, from his review in the *Herald Tribune* of January 27, 1950, of a New York Philharmonic performance of Anton Webern's Symphony:

"Anton Webern's Symphony for Chamber Orchestra, the novelty of last night's Philharmonic concert in Carnegie Hall, was 'advanced' music when first played here twenty years ago; and it still is. For all the world-wide spread of the twelve-tone technique that has taken place since then, it would be hard to find today five living adepts of it whose writing is so firm and so sophisticated as Webern's was. The audience effect of this work attested also to its vitality. Not only were repeated bows taken by the conductor, Dimitri Mitropoulos, and his excellent musicians. There was actually booing in the hall, a phenomenon almost unknown at the Philharmonic.

"The piece itself offends, as it delights, by its delicacy, transparency, and concentration. The first movement, for all its canonic rigor, is something of an ultimate in pulverization—star dust at the service of sentiment. Each instrument plays just one note, at most two; then another carries on the theme. The theme itself is a row of tones isolated from one another by scale skips. The texture is thin, too. One note at a time, just occasionally two or three, is the rule of its instrumental utterance. And yet the piece has a melodic and expressive consistency. It is clearly about something and under no temptation to fidget. Its form, I may add, is roughly that of a binary, or Scarlatti-type sonata; and its rhythmic pulse, save for a few retards in the second movement, is steady.

"This movement (there are only two) is a set of variations on the work's whole twelve-tone row, first stated completely at this poin. Rhythm is broken up into asymmetrical fragments. The melodic pulverization is less fine, however, than that of the first movement. Occasionally an instrument will articulate as many as eight or ten notes at a stretch. Some of these are even repeated notes. Metrical fragmentation has taken the place of melodic. The sonorous texture becomes even thinner at the end than anything one has heard previously. A tiny sprinkle of sounds; two widely spaced ones on the harp; and the vaporization is complete.

"There is every reason to believe the Philharmonic's reading of this tiny but ever so tough work to have been correct. Musicians following the score could question only the size here and there of some minute crescendo. The rendering was clear, clean, tonally agreeable, and expressive. Expressive of exactly what would be difficult to say, as it is of any work. Nevertheless, consistency and self-containment, ever the signs of expressive concentration, were present to the ear, just as they are to the eye reading the score. Once again there was cause to be grateful to Mr. Mitropoulos for his assiduity toward neglected distinction and for his enormous loyalty to the text of a work rare, complex, and in every way difficult. The rest of the program, standard stuff, sounded gross beside Webern's spun steel. Robert Casadesus played a Beethoven concerto in businesslike fashion, with dispatch and efficiency. A Rachmaninoff piece gave the conductor the conventional odds," etc.

Here in Mr. Thomson's neat review is a wonderfully concentrated and articulate example of what is wrong with modern music. One cannot miss the historical, esthetic, and social implications, particularly the picture of musicians following the score and questioning, here and there, "only the size of some minute crescendo." This sort of thing suggests caricature, as does the whole review. Consider the descriptive details: "asymmetrical fragments" . . . "melodic pulverization" . . . "metrical fragmentation" . . . "vaporization" . . . "a tiny sprinkle of sounds" . . . "spun steel" . . . etc.!

Actually, it is a superb piece of modern music appreciation, which is what makes it such an instructive document.

Pulverization, fragmentation, and vaporization are undoubtedly all present in Webern's little symphony, just as Mr. Thomson says. Nor are they applicable to Webern alone. They are characteristic, more or less, of most modern music, if not always so spectacularly, so obviously, or so exclusively. They represent what has happened to music. It is more than decadence. It is decomposition.

No one understands the contemporary composer better than his fellow composer, and none has pilloried this kind of music better than Hindemith:

"Still another group," he writes, "in an attempt to replace with an apparent rationality what is lacking morally, develops an over-sublimated technique which produces images of emotions that are far removed from any emotional experiences a relatively normal human being ever has. In doing so they advocate the esoteric *art pour l'art,* the followers of which they can only be emotional imps, monsters, or snobs.

"All these composers forget one important fact: music, as we practice it, is, in spite of its trend toward abstraction, a form of communication between the author and the consumer of his music. If with the method just described we try to push the listener into the background, the picture will be filled with something less pleasant than the dullest ignorance of a dumb group of listeners: our own selfishness. William H. Vanderbilt's maxim, 'The public be damned' would seem to be one of those composers' working rules; or else they claim that audiences have to rubber-stamp whatever they deem necessary to dump upon them; or, finally, they may say: 'The present world does not understand my music, but in two hundred years people will be mature enough to follow me."

"Even if in exceptional cases it may happen that composers are discovered who were never heard in their lifetime two hundred years previous, this attitude is utterly un-realistic, since it neglects one of the main reasons for artistic communication: the altruistic desire to present something of one's own to one's fellow man.

"An artist would be justified in retiring into this unpro-ductive resignation only if he were convinced that he had done everything in his power to make himself understood by his contemporaries. If he cannot succeed in doing so in one form or another, there will be very slight chance that pos-terity will recognize him as a great genius. It is more likely, however, that his composing is, except for himself, of no value to any one living either now or two hundred years hence." [2]

The contemporary composer justifies his retirement by the familiar rationalization about the laziness of audiences, the evils of commercialism, and what he likes to think of as the "managerial conspiracy" against him. He buttresses it with the flimsy legend of the misunderstood composer, the genius ahead of his time.

But composers are not unintelligent, and it is a safe bet that Hindemith is not the only one who has seen through rationalization to the truth. They are stuck, however, with their calling. In their careers they have passed the point of no return. As miniature emperors exhibiting themselves in the little-understood realm of serious music they prudently refrain from pointing out, even to each other, that they are not wearing any clothes.

THE COMPOSER'S DILEMMA

∻

THE contemporary composer is a frustrated fellow.

Society pins upon him its hopes of cultural continuity. Through grants, fellowships, commissions, and prizes—in Europe through subsidies—it encourages him to compose. But it withholds the awards of approbation, admiration, enthusiasm, and affection without which all other awards are empty.

Performers look to him for an enrichment of the repertoire, for something to ease the tedium of unending repetition of aging staples, and to rescue the art from the museum. They commission sonatas, concertos, and symphonies. They even play them. What comes of it? Novelties, briefly discussed, quickly discarded and forgotten!

Other composers assure him of the quality of his music and the excellence of the cause. They write expertly in trade magazines and scholarly periodicals about his style, his invention, his sources and his development. But what they write is little noted outside the profession.

Because real enthusiasm is lacking, the composer damns them all, the audience for its lazy preference for the familiar, the performer for his slavish catering to his audiences' tastes, his fellow composer for composing the inferior music which has given modern music a bad name. He compares them all with their counterparts of the past and concludes that they have changed for the worse.

In fact, they have changed less than he. It is not the world that has withdrawn from the composer, but the composer who has withdrawn from the world. The composer has only himself to blame if he finds the stratosphere too thin for comfort. He is there of his own choice.

"Clearly," says Honegger, "the composer is no longer what he was. Practitioner, as harpsichordist, organist, or violinist, he knew the rules of composition and composed in order to enrich his repertoire. Then—and here one must emphasize the distinction—the public had an appetite for novelty. Thus it was with Haydn, Telemann, Handel, and many others. And this explains their creative prolificness. They were simply craftsmen who worked according to the well-established rules. Many of their scores are so much alike that it is difficult to distinguish between them." [1] *

The contemporary composer may regard them with envy, but he would hardly accept the conditions under which they worked, or the stylistic conformity resulting from composition "according to the well-established rules." This would mean giving up the prestige and privilege won for him in the nineteenth century by masterpieces treasured for stylistic individuality and immortal inspiration.

The rise in the composer's station in life from village organist and court musician to unfettered genius was accomplished by men who neither observed nor made rules, and whose compositions are celebrated for the ease with which they can be distinguished from the work of other men, including their contemporaries.

The writer of popular music is free of this weight of the past, uninhibited by the serious composer's implicit obliga-

* *Je suis compositeur,* by Arthur Honegger. Copyright by Editions du Conquistador, Paris, 1951.

tion to aspire to timelessness. Like the older composers of whom Honegger speaks, he composes in order to enrich a repertoire, to give bands something to play and singers something to sing. Like theirs, his scores and improvisations are often so much like those of his colleagues that it is difficult to distinguish among them.

In short, he works, as did the older composers, in a style. It is the style of his time. He works according to well-established rules. These are simply the conventions established by popular taste. In observing them the popular composer automatically writes music that is of his time. In ignoring them, the serious composer automatically writes music that is not.

He cannot help himself. He is identified with a tradition that commends, not popularity, but significance; not identification with a common style, but an individual style; not the impersonal voice of society but the intimate voice of his inspiration. He dare not be popular, for popular music is assumed to be synonymous with light or easy music, and therefore inferior. The contemporary composer is, by definition, serious. His tradition requires, not success, but greatness.

His unpopularity is rendered tolerable only by his and society's faith in the legend that audiences have traditionally proved incapable of appreciating contemporary music. The rationalization is convenient both for society and the composer, but it cannot alter the composer's fate. In writing for a posterity of whose physiognomy he cannot be certain, the composer will hardly find an audience in the present, and is unlikely, as Hindemith has remarked, to find one in the future.

Such is the composer's dilemma. He cannot write popularly without hazarding the respect accorded him as a writer of serious music. He cannot write seriously without forsaking popularity. The implications of this can be followed in the careers of the individual composers.

Those who have stuck most faithfully to the concept of progress, and have written the most progressive music, such composers as Schönberg, Berg, Webern, Bartok, Hindemith, and the post-war Stravinsky, have been the most greatly respected in the profession but have made the least progress with the public.

Those who have courted the public, such composers as Weill and Menotti, have enjoyed some measure of popular success but little esteem in the profession. Their talent is acknowledged, but they are not thought of as significant contributors to musical history, and the non-significance of their music is duly emphasized by the critics and their fellow composers. Nor have they achieved a popularity comparable to that of really popular composers.

The effect of this equivocal situation upon the individual composer has been well described by one who can speak from two-fold personal experience, Ernst Krenek. In his *Self-Portrait* [13] Mr. Krenek writes:

"When I contemplate my life work thus far, it occurs to me that I have been motivated by two forces whose visible effects often appear to contradict each other. Early in my career I felt myself drawn to the idea of pure, uncompromising creation, independent of the currents of the time, and indeed often expressly opposed to them. At the same time I was susceptible to the temptation to achieve practical results in this world. . . ."

The full import of the contradiction was revealed to Mr. Krenek by the success of his opera *Jonny spielt auf* in Europe in the late twenties. He had already—following his first impulse—established a reputation for himself as a radical young man. But in this opera, due partly to its singular subject matter, and partly to a voluntary reaction against his own wild radicalism, he "returned to the idiom of tonality and the cantilena of Puccini . . . the whole thing spiced with elements of jazz."

The success, says Mr. Krenek, was "immediate and overpowering. In the following two years the piece was performed in more than a hundred theaters in all of Europe, and in many of them it held on in the repertoire for some time."

But it was a bitter-sweet triumph. In Vienna a few years later he found himself welcome in neither the modernist nor the popular camp. As he tells it:

"My romantic compositions enjoyed some success, since their traditional language exercised a certain attractive force. But since these works were not absolutely flat and ordinary they could not easily compete with compositions in which inherited materials were uncritically employed.

"The modernists, on the other hand, regarded these works of mine more or less as curiosities. Thus they vegetated in that small area in which their limited popularity coincided with the moderate interest they excited as singular utterances of a composer who had once been progressive. . . .

"I have the impression that the success of '*Jonny spielt auf*' nullified in the public mind everything that I had thus far achieved. Observers who had been sympathetic to my earlier daring experiments were disillusioned, as though I had made a business out of music. This was not, however, the case, and so it was inevitable that I should disillusion those who expected that *Jonny* would be followed by sensational hits in the same style. The result was that I soon found myself sitting between two stools."

This is the answer to those who argue that the solution to the problem of modern music is for the contemporary composer to come down out of his ivory tower and write a couple of good tunes. It is not so simple. Whether the composer comes down of his own accord, as happens from time to time in free societies, or is hauled down, as happens in totalitarian societies, the result is failure, or at best disappointment.

In the Soviet Union an attempt has been made to resolve the composer's dilemma by decree. He has been told to get down to earth and write more popularly or forego the privileges to which he is entitled as an intellectual ornament of Soviet society. The effort is a failure, as it was bound to be.

Not even a system as autocratic as that of the Soviet Union can control the evolution of social forces or, for that matter, escape them; and the evolution of music is inseparable from social evolution. Those who have modestly undertaken to direct the cultural destiny of the Russian masses proceed from the identical error that so confuses musical thought in the Western world. This is the assumption that music is made by composers rather than by societies. But in the Soviet Union the inevitably unsatisfactory result is a more serious matter.

Those who act as custodians of serious music in the Western world can go on kidding themselves as long as society makes no objections and even acquiesces to the extent of supporting the illusion with tolerance and money. Those who control serious music in the Soviet Union are responsible to state authorities of notoriously unindulgent disposition.

Since in the Soviet Union the composer is supported by the state, he is expected to serve the state. The latter, not unreasonably, is disinclined to regard "ultimate pulverization . . . star dust at the service of sentiment" as a notable contribution to the edification and enlightenment of a classless society.

But neither is it willing to fall behind the capitalist West in the production of what has been inherited as a tradition of excellence in one of the great arts. To a nation not wanting in intellectual self-consciousness and cultural insecurity it is no small matter to be able to match Bartok, Schönberg, and Webern with Prokofiev, Shostakovich, and Khatchaturian. Such assets in the competition for cultural esteem and prestige cannot be discarded lightly.

The Soviet problem, however, is to equate these prestige assets with the musical requirements of Soviet society. There is no getting around the fact that little is written by the famous Soviet composers that the Soviet people could not easily forego. To attempt to solve the problem by ordering the composer to write serious music more popularly is a clear case of trying to have the cake and eat it too.

The Western composer cannot leave his ivory tower without denying the myth of his cultural superiority, without hazarding his status as a serious composer. A totalitarian government cannot compel him to leave it without subjecting him to the same jeopardy. By forcing him to compromise himself as a serious composer, it requires that he dissipate those very qualities that earn him respect both at home and abroad and thus constitute a large part of his value.

And in vain! Men of the background, experience, and intellectual disposition of a Shostakovich can as little write for contemporary Russia as America's serious composers can write for contemporary America. They can accede to a certain inhibition of their intellectual habits and their natural musical impulses, but not much more. The result, lacking spontaneity and conviction, can never be more than a pathetic hybrid.

All this is quite aside from the monstrousness of assuming that any government can impose a certain kind of music upon its subjects. It can impose, to be sure, in the sense that it requires that certain music be written, played, and listened to. But it cannot make that music stick. It cannot make it a people's music.

A society will create its own music, for of all arts it is the most immediately human and the most irresistibly spontaneous. It cannot be ordered or dictated—or better, a taste for it cannot be ordered. Neither the Soviet composer, complying with the directives of his government, nor the Western composer, complying with the dictates of his inspiration, can create a Soviet or an American or a European music. A society's music is determined, not by what appeals to a government, or to a composer, but by what appeals to society, and it will have its roots in what society sings and dances to. The only effective prerogative of a totalitarian government is suppression.

Our contemporary Western society has produced and developed its own musical expression in a wonderfully natural and spontaneous way—and without consultation with composers, critics, and musicologists. There is every reason to believe that its appeal is universal or close to it. If the Iron Curtain were lifted, no propaganda could stop the eastward sweep of American popular music to the Pacific.

This has nothing to do with serious music. The contemporary composer likes to talk about writing the music of his own time, about reflecting through his superior musical intellect the society of which he feels himself to be a part. But his music is modern only in the sense that it is written in the present. It is identifiable as such only in the sense that it resembles, more or less, the music of other men of similar aspirations. It expresses nothing but his own incapacity to express anything.

It is not the music of modern society, and it never will be. Nor would society approve if it were. Society prefers to think that there is something better than popular music, and it looks to the serious composer to provide it. The composer may draw upon popular sources, as the saying goes, but he must submit them to intellectual processing. The thumbscrews of modern harmony and the rack of modern orchestration are considered an essential ritual in the preparation of popular musical elements for a condition of cultural grace.

This works, in a way, to the composer's advantage. Since

the assumption that serious music is better than popular music is generally accepted by laymen, society flatters him with greater respect, if not with greater affection, than it bestows upon the men whose songs it sings. But it also works against him, since society is little pleased with his performance, and has no other choice than to take him on faith.

In short, the puzzlement and frustration that trouble both composer and listener in their efforts to understand the unpopularity of modern music, and the characteristics that make it unpopular, are derived, not simply from a failure to solve the problem of getting composer and listener together, but from a failure to recognize that the problem is insoluble.

In free societies the audience may complain about the music, and the composer about the audience; in totalitarian societies the state may order the composer to write more popularly, and the composer may complain about the ills of bureaucracy. In either case the fact is overlooked that the composer cannot help himself. He is both the beneficiary and the victim of a concept of musical history that proceeds from the assumption of music as the product of composers rather than of societies.

It is true that in highly developed musical societies certain composers have stood out and seemed to make musical history. But this occurs at the end rather than the beginning of cultural phases, and is valid only as long as the product meets the approval of the society for which it is produced. The symbol of cultural prosperity is not an individual, nor a group of individuals, but a style. It is society's verdict, as expressed in a style, not the composer's inspiration, as expressed in a masterpiece, that determines the course of musical history.

This has not been true of serious music since before the First World War, and society has forgotten, or chosen to overlook, the fact that it ever was. Musical history and musical criticism have made the error of concentrating on composers rather than on society. While critics and scholars have been studying and discussing modern music, sociological developments in the past thirty years have had far more influence upon musical history than Schönberg's discovery of the twelve-tone row or Stravinsky's discovery of Pergolesi.

Consequently, both criticism and history have overlooked the one fact about the contemporary composer that is of any real importance to the understanding of modern music: he is obsolete.

COMPOSER AND CRITIC

❖

MUSICAL history assigns to the music critic an ignominious role. The prototype is Wagner's Sixtus Beckmesser, the Meistersinger pedant who harps on the rules and defends an old system with which he is familiar against a new system with which he is not. He is the Philistine pitted in benighted opposition to the forces of progress and enlightenment.

The late Ernest Newman summed up the situation tidily in the introduction to his edition of Chorley's *Thirty Years' Musical Recollections*:[14]

"It is difficult," he wrote, "for the musical critic to achieve any immortality except one of opprobrium. He is remembered solely by his few misses; his many hits are not counted to him. The reason is obvious. If he talks sense, his views become the commonplaces of musical opinion, and no one thinks of crediting him in particular with them. If he talks nonsense, this is regarded as peculiarly his own, and is sure to be brought up against him by some musical biographer or other who wants to intensify the sympathetic atmosphere surrounding his hero by showing how sadly sympathy was lacking to him while he was alive."

One has to look no farther than Mr. Newman himself to see how this works. In the introduction to his edition of Berlioz's *Memoirs*[15] he wrote: "Thousands of people who have

not the least idea how much good sense Chorley and Hanslick talked about music remember them for one or two mistakes they made about Wagner." As Wagner's biographer
this same Mr. Newman referred to Hanslick as a simpleton,
and once went so far as to denounce him as "the most colossal ignoramus and charlatan who ever succeeded in imposing
himself on an editor as a musical critic." [16]

This illustrates the problem nicely. As Wagner's biographer, Mr. Newman was writing a success story. Success was
won against opposition, and was recognized as having been
good for society. Therefore opposition was bad, and those
who practiced it were villains or fools.

As a critic, speaking for Chorley and Berlioz, Mr. Newman
knew that it was not so simple. He knew that the critics
about whom he wrote were well-informed and honest men
who happened to hold opinions contrary to the consensus of
society. Since society thinks that society is right, it must also
assume that the critics were wrong.

Thus Mr. Newman's perspective changed as he moved
from his position as critic to his position as biographer. In the
latter role he committed precisely the sin of distortion which,
as a critic, he accused other biographers of committing. It
seems to be a matter of whose bull is being gored. Historically speaking, society's bull has been the composer, and society has taken sides accordingly when composer and critic
were in conflict.

It all depends on whether or not one accepts what Hindemith has called "the evolutionist's theory of music's increasing development toward higher goals." [2] Hindemith himself,
like most composers, finds this theory untenable. But musical
society accepts it without qualification—and thus has no
choice but to condemn the critic as an obstructionist.

If, however, one believes, as most composers do, that serious music has been in decline for anywhere up to a century

and a half, there is nothing for it but to congratulate the critics who pointed out, at each step along the way, that music
was headed toward disaster. Contemporary composers would
be the last to offer such congratulations, publicly, at least. It
would put bad ideas into the heads of contemporary critics.
The latter are now intimidated and docile, polite even when
offended. It is in the composer's interest to keep them that
way.

The evolutionist's theory has been spectacularly docu-
mented recently in Nicolas Slonimsky's *Lexicon of Musical
Invective*,[17] an "anthology of critical assaults upon composers since the time of Beethoven." The animating purpose
of this book, the author tells us, "is to demonstrate that music
is an art in progress, and that objections leveled at every musical innovator are all derived from the same psychological
inhibition, which may be described as Non-Acceptance of the
Unfamiliar."

From his own analysis of the anthology, Mr. Slonimsky
even deduces a time-table for the assimilation of unfamiliar
music by the public and the critics. "It takes," he says, "ap-
proximately twenty years to make an artistic curiosity out of a
modernistic monstrosity, and another twenty to elevate it to
a masterpiece." Elsewhere he refers to this as "the law of a
forty-year lag in the integral acceptance of a modern masterpiece."

That this little book has had the anticipated mollifying effect upon those who might otherwise speak up about modern
music was indicated by the obliging comment of Mephisto in
Musical America: "I recommend this '*Schimpflexikon*' to all
who are prone to jump to conclusions about new music, and
particularly to those who insist upon measuring the present
and the future with the yardstick of the past."

As if there were, or ever had been, anything else to measure it by!

All the basic source material of popular historical distortion is present or plainly implicit in this *Lexicon of Musical Invective.*

There is, first, the assumption that the history of music is a history of continuous progress, onward and upward. And then, by implication at least, there is the corollary that progress is to be construed as meaning that music has been getting better and better. If this were not assumed to be true, and if music, instead of getting better and better, had been getting worse and worse, then the critics who disparaged the innovators must have been right. Mr. Slonimsky's position, like that of most musical historians, is that they were wrong.

As a defender of "modern monstrosities" this is the only position he can take. To admit that the authors of invective may have been anything but benighted would be to question the foundation on which the toleration of modern music is based. This is the assumption that music is an art in progress. Thus the legend of critical benightedness persists despite the fact that the majority of those who propagate it would readily admit that, as between Beethoven and Wagner, the former was the greater.

Or one does as Ernst Krenek does in his *Self-Portrait* [13] and pleads extenuating circumstances.

"The term 'progress,' " he says, "can be applied to art only if one attributes to it a different meaning from that which it has in reference to material accomplishments. While there is no doubt that railroads are better today than they were a hundred years ago, since it is possible to gauge accurately their capacity and efficiency, no reasonable person will agree that the history of the symphony from Mozart to Mahler represents a similar progress.

"The perfect work of art can never be surpassed by later achievements, since its perfection can be measured only within its own frame of reference. . . . When we speak of

progress in respect to art we mean only that various phenomena follow one another in point of time, without wishing to
imply that what came later was necessarily better than what
went before."

This is rather like saying that one should not consider one
vintage better than another because the two were exposed to
different weather conditions, or that one should not find one
wine better than another because it was grown in a more favorable locality. And it has a hollow ring coming from a man
who says in the same breath: "No one today will question the
opinion that Beethoven's *Eroica* is more significant than his
First Symphony and that it represents enormous progress in
the growth of the master." Would Mr. Krenek, who has just
said that "the perfect work of art can never be surpassed by
later achievements," deny that he considers the *Eroica* the
better symphony of the two?

Then there is the legend, or law, as Mr. Slonimsky calls it,
of the "forty-year lag in the integral acceptance of a modern
masterpiece." It is not commonly articulated thus precisely,
but the assumption that new works of quality are slow to catch
on is generally accepted. There will be occasion later to ex-
amine this fable more closely. It may suffice for the present
to note that even *Le sacre du printemps,* the example chosen
by Mr. Slonimsky to support his estimate, can also be used
to refute it.

The premiere of *Le sacre* in Paris in 1913 was a famous
scandal. As usual in such instances, there was more to the
turbulence than just popular indignation at music of hitherto
unexampled violence. But history has dramatized the scandal
and overlooked the fact that the work had a popular success
when given in concert form in Paris less than a year later.
Moreover, *Le sacre* enjoyed greater popularity and critical
esteem in the twenties and early thirties than it enjoys now.

Often cited by others as an example of the time it takes a

modern masterpiece to catch on is *Wozzeck.* Here again the facts give a different picture. *Wozzeck* was first given in Berlin in 1925. In the following ten years it was given 166 times in twenty-nine cities and in five languages. Even the first hearing of the music, a concert of excerpts under the direction of Hermann Scherchen in Frankfurt in June, 1923, resulted, according to Berg's pupil and biographer, Willi Reich, in a sensational success. "From this day onward," Mr. Reich has written, "Berg and his *Wozzeck* were famous." [18]

In both cases we have to do with controversial works whose success was, and still is, more a matter of critical esteem than of popular enthusiasm. How does the legend stand up to the immediate and enduring successes of such works as *The Firebird* and *Petrouchka*? What is one to say of *Aïda, Otello, Falstaff, Cavalleria Rusticana, La Bohème, Tosca,* and even *Pelléas et Mélisande,* all of which were also immediately successful? Not to mention the Wagner music-dramas, the Brahms symphonies, and Richard Strauss's tone poems and early operas!

But the legend persists despite the readily available refutatory evidence. Its general acceptance is the critic's knottiest problem—and not the less so because as often as not he believes it himself. It dooms him to be a writer of music appreciation, a commentator rather than critic.

To challenge contemporary music, according to the legend, is to be an obstructionist. It is also tempting fate. Posterity may not endorse the judgment. The contemporary critic, a conservative at heart, hedges his bets accordingly. To challenge the legend itself is to challenge popular superstition, and is even more hazardous than making a pass now and then at contemporary music.

Thus the critic is as much the victim of superstition as the lay listener, and usually as unwittingly. This explains that lack of any sense of adventure which has caused music criticism of this century to be so remarkably uninteresting. The calcification of the repertoire in the first decade of the century seems to have coincided with a calcification of society's thinking about music and musical history. It could not have happened at a worse time.

Wagner had conquered. Strauss had followed up his tone poems with *Salomé, Elektra,* and *Der Rosenkavalier.* Stravinsky's ballets were the rage. Debussy had triumphed with *Pelléas et Mélisande,* Ravel with *Daphnis and Chloe,* Charpentier with *Louise,* and Puccini with *Madame Butterfly.* It looked like anything but a dead end. The Philistines were in flight. The present was glorious and the future bright. Critical romance was in flower.

Now, forty years later, the flower appears to have been made of nearly imperishable wax. There has been no original thinking about music since then; at least, no original thinking has excited sufficient interest or proven sufficiently influential to shake society's faith in the conventions of critical thought as they existed in 1910.

Among these conventions the evolutionist's theory of progress was outstanding. The masterpieces of the nineteenth century had prevailed in the face of militant opposition. The "verdict of posterity" had fallen. It was: "All glory to the masterpieces and all ignominy to those who had opposed them!" The historical implications seemed to be that progress is inevitable and good, that opposition is ill-fated and bad.

The definitiveness of the verdict and the universality of its acceptance forty years ago were such that henceforth few critics dared or were even disposed to challenge it. Ever since then, criticism has observed certain undocumented but well-understood bounds, among which the sanctity of the masterpieces and the assumption of infinite progress are the most clearly defined.

Generally speaking, contemporary criticism is original or

contentious only within these bounds. It is permissible, for instance, to argue the pros and cons of certain ways of playing or appreciating Beethoven's last quartets, but it is nonconformist to suggest that they may not, after all, have been Beethoven's greatest works. One may accept or reject Wieland Wagner's staging of his grandfather's music-dramas, but it is no longer good form to quarrel with the operas themselves, even if one does not happen to like them. One may prefer one contemporary composer to another, and even find fault here and there with the most famous. But it is unthinkable to dismiss modern music as a fraud, and it is a blasphemy to suggest that the road to bankruptcy began with Beethoven.

The critics of the nineteenth century used to dare this sort of dogmatic opinion, and their targets responded in kind. It made for lively exchanges of opinion. This was criticism—personal, biased, passionate, and fallible. What matters who was right and who was wrong? Who can judge, even today? Are we to assume that our present view of the nineteenth century represents the ultimate and indisputably correct word on the subject? Must it be forever binding on everyone?

Contemporary musical society conducts itself as if it assumed that the answer were yes. Contemporary criticism conforms. The existence of right and wrong in the judgment of music is acknowledged, and nobody wants to be wrong. What was right and what was wrong in the past is held to be established. About the present one only knows that music must go on, that it must progress, and that tolerance, temperance, and ambiguity are the parts of wisdom for those who sit in judgment.

Such is the dogma. Its observance is plainly more dogmatic than the assertive criticism of the past which is now denounced as dogmatism. It is certainly less interesting.

Faced with the two-fold calcification of the repertoire

and of critical thought about it, professional and lay criticism concentrate on appreciation and the judgment of performance. The composer, however, dare not be so acquiescent. He has not escaped the calcification of thought as it affects his position in society. He benefits from it. But he cannot accept the calcification of the repertoire, which exposes him to unequal competition with the popular masters and leaves him the provider of unwelcome novelties whose sole purpose is to reassure society that the art is still progressing, if, for the moment, unattractively.

He argues, and not without some logic, that a musical society committed to the evolutionist's theory should put the theory into practice and take his music to its heart as its own. Society applauds the theory but not the music. It concedes that the music should be heard, but feels constrained only to listen to it, not to like it.

To like modern music, it is assumed, will be the privilege of posterity. Society feels that it has discharged its responsibility by giving contemporary music a more gracious hearing than was sometimes accorded, in their own time, to the masterpieces society now enjoys. For the composer this is not enough.

The resultant frustration has made him articulate, at least in prose. Indeed, it is probably no exaggeration to say that the composer has taken over the functions of creative criticism defaulted by the professional critics when they accepted the verdict of 1910 as final. The composer alone contests the verdict and insists that the case is not closed. This he must do, for his own music is a contradiction of the verdict, through and through.

Everything that he has written since the First World War in prose and in music, represents a rejection of, or a rebellion against, the musical esthetics of the nineteenth century. These are precisely the esthetics which are the substance of conventional thinking about music. They are the esthetics that inspired the composition of that music which contemporary audiences still like best and which contemporary critics still prize as the pinnacle of musical achievement.

The composer can and does put his finger on esthetic and technical blemishes in the pillars of the standard repertoire that the audience neither notices nor is disposed to look for. And he does it with critically sound esthetic and technical argument. He has produced the only important original and contentious criticism this century has produced.

This should not be surprising. The composer knows that as long as the musical public sees no sin in Wagner, as long as it is held spellbound by Richard Strauss, it is unlikely to turn to modern music for musical sustenance. The composer has become a critic in self-defense. It is a role to which he is suited by endowment. As a composer he is inclined to confuse inclination and talent. As a critic he has more talent than inclination. He has never realized how much even his composition is a species of criticism.

Everything he does is of critical rather than creative origin, his music as well as his prose. And he is a good critic—about everything except contemporary music, sometimes about everything except his own music. The professional critics have little to show that can compare in originality of thought and keenness of insight with the books of Lambert, Hindemith, Krenek, Schönberg, Stravinsky, Honegger, Milhaud, Copland, Thomson, Sessions, Moore, and a number of others.

This is an odd state of affairs. It is not, after all, the composer's part to be a critic. In healthier times the roles were properly distributed. The composer composed and the critic wrote criticism. Some composers in the nineteenth century, to be sure, worked at criticism, but with the exception of Berlioz and Debussy they were not notably good at it. And they worked at a time when the intellectualization of music had already reached a point where composers were beginning to sense the need of explaining themselves and their contemporaries by means more precise than their music.

The present excellence of composer criticism is symbolic of the time. Both neo-classicism and atonality are products of critical reflection. They derive, not from any spontaneous creative impulse, as classicism did in Mozart's time, or monodic harmony in Monteverdi's, but from esthetic calculation and conviction, and from preoccupation with technical problems.

Small wonder, then, that the composers of the most prosaic music the world has ever known should prove capable of articulate prose and emerge as the best critics the composing profession has ever produced!

It illustrates the difference between the composer-revolutionary of today and the composer-revolutionary of a hundred, or a hundred and fifty years ago. Both Wagner and Beethoven spoke for generations that shared their views and sympathized with the passions and aspirations expressed in their music. Opposition came from the critics. Today's composer-revolutionary rebels against a generation that finds nothing of itself in his music. And he has the critics on his side. Of real opposition, which is the evidence of vitality, there is none.

The composer is really this generation's reactionary critic, a fellow who takes a poor view of the musical temper of his time. What distinguishes him from the reactionary critic of the nineteenth century is the fact that his criticism excites no indignation. He is insufficiently identified with society to render his opinions disturbing.

One of the most telling evidences of the obsolescence of serious music is the fact that critical controversy is no more. Stravinsky, Bartok, Schönberg, and Berg all excited a spate of reactionary indignation in the early years of the century,

but it was short-lived. None of them caught on with a large
public, as Wagner, Strauss, and Bruckner had caught on
before them, nor did they attract a similarly numerous and
partisan following.

The result, as far as criticism is concerned, has been a droll
reversal of positions. Where the critic formerly stood off both
composer and public in defense of conservative views in
which he believed passionately, he now allies himself with
the composer in defense of music for which he has little enthusiasm.

He may dislike individual compositions, and say so; but
he says it politely, and more in sorrow than in anger. He will
not say how bad he really thinks it is. This would expose
him to the charge of being destructive. A destructive critic,
according to the indulgent mores of contemporary musical
society, is a villain. The critic is rather inclined to agree. He
has accepted the chamber of commerce injunction: If you
can't boost, don't knock. It is the end of criticism.

When the composer was doing well the critic could afford
to attack him, for business was healthy, and controversy was
good for it. Each was immune from serious damage. The
odds favored the composer as long as he could please the
public. The critic who attacked him made enemies, but he
also made readers.

Now, with the composer doing badly, the critic tends, as
a fellow professional, to take his side. Critic and composer
are dependent upon one another for survival. Neither is
strong enough to withstand a series of heavy blows from the
other. In effect, critic and composer are, as Mr. Thomson has
suggested they should be, banded together as co-professionals
in a conspiracy to defend the faith.

History's disparagement of the role of the critic in the past
actually makes this change of position popular and assures

it the stamp of social approval. Today's critic is regarded as an enlightened champion of the new and the unfamiliar, the courageous defender of the composer underdog. By defending modern music in principle and occasionally disparaging it in detail the critic accommodates both the superstition of progress and the distaste of the modern audience for modern music.

There is a good deal of hypocrisy in this. The critic's position is fashionable, the only one which society, with its present concept of musical history, can approve. In fact, while priding himself on his enlightenment and his courage, the critic displays little of either. It may have taken courage to defend Wagner a hundred years ago, when opposition was real and emotional. It took courage to oppose him, too, for the enthusiasts were numerous, and inspired by evangelical faith and fervor. Today it takes no courage to defend anybody, since nobody is really opposed. The contemporary critic defending modern music goes off to joust with a windmill.

He is the effete descendant of a warrior clan decimated in battle and discredited by history. His reading of the family archives has encouraged him to avoid the mistakes of his forefathers and to seek an alliance with the enemy. Since both composer and critic are aware that the arrangement is not entirely honorable, they fight a sham battle now and then to keep up appearances. But for the most part they fight together against the public—not openly under flags, but furtively, like signal-exchanging partners in a poker game.

As usual, the critic is wrong. Having seen what happened to critics who pointed to faults in composers now remembered for their virtues, he looks for virtues in composers likely to be remembered for their want of any virtue at all. Or, to put it differently, the critic opposed new music when it was good, or at least when there was still good in it, and now compounds the error by defending it when there is little in it to defend.

Serious music has moved into the museum, and the critics with it, there to act as curators of the masterpieces and judges of contemporary candidates for admission. In this latter role they distinguish themselves by an indulgence assumed to be enlightened. The legitimacy of the assumption is doubtful.

Nor can it be left at that. For the new music, defended, or at least tolerated, by the contemporary critic is not even the real music of his time. While he has sought to persuade himself and his readers that serious music is still an art in progress, the generation of which he is a member has produced, in American jazz, a new art music shaped by the intellectual and emotional character of twentieth-century society.

The reactionary critic in the nineteenth century opposed the new music of his time, as he had a good right as a critic to do. He did not like it, and he said so. But he knew, at least, what that new music was. The progressive critic of the present, blissfully preoccupied with the will-of-the-wisp of musical progress accomplished in an intellectual vacuum, has failed to recognize the real new music of his time when he heard it.

He has consistently confused inspiration and inclination. As an amateur and connoisseur of European music from Bach to Bartok, he is interested in the continuity of the tradition and in making his own contribution. He has ignored as unworthy any music of different traditional origin. This has prompted him to overestimate, wishfully, uninspired new music that calls itself serious and to disparage, apprehensively, new music of less traditional physiognomy but real inspiration, notably jazz.

What he espouses is not so much a music as a concept of

music, the notion that only music identified with the European tradition need be taken seriously and that such serious music must somehow be perpetuated. In this respect he resembles the composer. Like the composer, he cannot abandon the tradition without also forsaking the respect which his identification with it earns for him in the serious music community. When Mr. Thomson speaks of "a conspiracy to defend the faith" he is probably doing so as a composer rather than as a critic, and what he says may be taken, in a sense, as an admonition. As such it is superfluous.

If the critic is to survive as anything other than musicologist and appraiser of performances, then he must have new music upon which to practice criticism. If the composer is to survive he must have critics to endorse his *bona fides*. Thus it is that the end of the European musical tradition finds composer and critic on the same side of the fence or, to put it more accurately, seated together out on the same limb.

There they are likely to stay for some time to come. Each has a saw in the form of his honest opinion of the other. But neither of them can use it without inviting his own destruction. Since both composers and critics are, for the most part, nothing if not intelligent, there is no reason to expect either of them to indulge in any such foolishness.

SUCCESS AND FAILURE

❖
❖ ❖
❖

THE most devastating single inhibiting factor standing in the way of spontaneous and honest judgment of modern music is the general acceptance, among professionals and laymen alike, of the fable that new serious music is never "understood" and appreciated in its own time.

This is the result of decades of popularized history and hack program note writing, both of which have consistently indulged in the sentimental dramatization of great composers' initial difficulties, subsequent economic and social setbacks, and occasional musical failures.

Nothing else has done so much to distort society's view of the relationship between composer and public. Nothing else has contributed so importantly to society's assumption that the present gap between composer and public is the normal relationship and that it always has been.

The factual materials upon which this distortion is based are familiar. There are, to begin with, the melancholy circumstances under which such composers as Mozart, Beethoven, Schubert, Schumann, and Chopin lived and died. Then there is the exultant quotation of derogatory criticism. And, finally, there is the unremittent reference to the initial failure of works now famous and popular.

In seeking to adjust the distortion as it affects our understanding of musical evolution, it is essential to separate the pertinent from the irrelevant. The circumstances of economic, physical, and mental stability under which man lived and died is, for instance, irrelevant. Society cannot be held responsible for the fact that a number of its composers have been bad business men. Nor can it be blamed for their want of physical or mental health.

Similarly, the fact that critics voiced objections which do not stand up against the test of time has no bearing upon the case. All that counts is how society reacted to this music when it was new. A composer's way is not—or, at least, it was not—made by critics, nor have ill-disposed critics been able to oppose effectively a good composer's progress. The only verdict that counts is the public's.

Thus the problem resolves itself into a simple question of success and failure. It should matter little to the student of evolution whether a composer died rich or poor, in good health or bad, or whether the balance of critical judgment was in his favor or not. Only the question of his popular success is important. Did the public for which he wrote like his music? Did it like it enough to demand more? Did his popularity influence the work of other composers?

Here the popular historical record has been distorted by the sentimental dramatization of such famous failures as those of *The Barber of Seville*, *La Traviata*, *Carmen*, *Madame Butterfly*, *Le sacre du printemps*, and the Franck symphony. Usually omitted in the accounts of these failures is the fact that every one of them became a great success within a few months of the unsuccessful premiere, sometimes within a few days, and that failure in most cases was due to extraneous and irrelevant circumstances, such as a bad performance, a series of stage accidents, or an intrigue.

The truth is that every great composer, without exception, has been appreciated, admired, applauded, and loved in his own time. Even those who died miserably died famous.

This runs so contrary to what the layman has been told in his music appreciation courses and in his program notes that he finds it difficult to believe. But believe it he must if he wishes to hear modern music in a correct perspective. And believe it he will if he reads history instead of program notes. As he is unlikely to go to the serious historical record, there is nothing for it but to bring the historical record to him.

Since Western music, in the orchestral and harmonic form in which it is familiar to us, may be said to have had its first great protagonist in Haydn (he is commonly referred to as "the father of the symphony," the distinctive form of Western orchestral music), it is appropriate to open the record at his name. Says his biographer, Karl Geiringer: [10]

"World fame it was indeed that came to Haydn while he worked in the solitude of Eszterhaza. His name traveled far beyond the borders of his own country, and in the whole of Europe there was hardly a music lover who did not know of and admire the works of Josef Haydn."

After Haydn's debut under Salomon's auspices at the Hanover Square Rooms in London on March 11, 1791, the foremost English critic and historian, Burney, spoke of an "electrical effect on all present" and of "such a degree of enthusiasm as almost amounted to frenzy." [10] Oxford University awarded him an honorary degree, and the conservative *Morning Chronicle* spoke of his "agitating modulations" and "larmoyant passages" and expressed the hope that Haydn might be "induced by our liberal welcome to take up his residence in England." [10]

At the premiere of *The Creation* in Vienna on April 29, 1798, "Twelve policemen and eighteen mounted guards were stationed to keep order in the walkways to the house. . . . The success was overwhelming and far beyond expectations. Most of the listeners may have felt like the Viennese correspondent of the *Neuer Teutscher Merkur*, who wrote: 'Three days have gone since that enrapturing evening, and still the music sounds in my ears and in my heart; still the mere memory of all the flood of emotions then experienced constricts my chest.' " [10]

Of the premiere of *The Seasons* three years later the correspondent of the *Allgemeine Musikalische Zeitung* wrote: "Silent reverence, amazement and loud enthusiasm alternated, for the powerful appearance of colossal visions, the immeasurable abundance of splendid ideas surprised and overwhelmed the boldest expectations." [10]

What celebrity and veneration might Mozart's have been had he lived as long as Haydn! As it was, the success of his operas was such that Haydn himself thought better of competing with him. A firsthand account of what this success amounted to is available to us in the accounts both of Mozart and of the Irish singer Michael Kelly.

Writing after the premiere of *The Marriage of Figaro*, in which he participated, Kelly wrote: "Never was anything so complete as the triumph of Mozart and his *Marriage of Figaro*." [19]

A few months later Mozart himself could write from Prague: "The one subject of conversation here is *Figaro*. Nothing is played, sung or whistled but *Figaro*; nobody goes to any opera but—*Figaro*; everlastingly *Figaro*!" [19]

At the premiere of *Don Giovanni* in Prague a year later, we read: "On Mozart's appearance in the orchestra he was greeted with enthusiastic applause and a triple flourish of trumpets, and the opera was accompanied from beginning to end with rapturous marks of approval." [19]

The legend of the "misunderstood composer," of the "Non-Acceptance of the Unfamiliar," begins properly, however, with Beethoven; but here, again, history is curiously at odds with the legend. When he was hardly more than thirty,

Beethoven could write: "My compositions bring me in a great deal, and I can say that I have more orders than I can execute. I have six or seven publishers for each one of my works and could have more if I chose. No more bargaining; I name my terms and they pay." [19]

Of his situation by the time he had reached the age of 45, Sir George Grove could say: "He had produced his latest and then greatest works under such favorable circumstances as no musician had ever before enjoyed. He had been feted and caressed by emperors and empresses and others of this world's great." [19]

The same writer, comparing the last illnesses of Schubert and Beethoven, writes of the latter: "Officious friends like Pasqualati sending him wine and delicacies; worshipping musicians like Hummel and Hiller coming to his death-bed as if to a shrine; his faithful attendants, Schindler, Hütten-brenner and Breuning waiting on his every word; the sense of a long life of honor and renown, of great works appreci-ated and beloved; the homage of distant countries expressed in the most substantial forms."

Even the Ninth Symphony was an instant success. One ac-count tells how the house was crowded and the music, espe-cially the symphony, "excited the greatest enthusiasm." [19] According to another and less restrained report, "the audience rose in salvo upon salvo of such enthusiasm as had never be-fore been aroused by any musical composition." [3] The faith-ful Schindler wrote next day in the conversation book: "The entire people is overwhelmed and shattered by the greatness of your works." [20]

As for Schubert, the poverty of his daily circumstances and the meanness of his death and interment have provided splendid fuel for fanciful biography, although, as Grove points out, "with his astonishing power of production the commonest care would have assured him a good living."

But even he, whose indolence in everything except composition prevented him from helping himself or helping others to help him, could not escape a considerable measure of contemporary fame and affection.

As Grove puts it: "We have been thus far particular to name the numbers and publishers of these works because they show conclusively how much Schubert's music was coming into demand. The list is a remarkable one, and will compare for extent and variety with that of most years of Beethoven's life."

On Schubert's contemporary, Carl Maria von Weber, the record is more definitive, particularly with respect to his masterpiece, *Der Freischütz*. Its premiere in Berlin in 1821 is described as follows in Grove:

"The 18th of June was as great a day of triumph as ever fell to the lot of a musician. The applause of a house filled to the very last seat was such as had never been heard before, in Germany, at any rate. That this magnificent homage was no outcome of party spirit was shown by the enduring nature of the success, and by the fact that it was the same wherever *Der Freischütz* was heard. No sooner had it been produced in Berlin than it was seized upon by nearly all the principal theaters in Germany."

Weber himself conducted a performance of *Der Freischütz* in Vienna on March 7, 1822, following which he wrote in his diary: "Conducted *Der Freischütz* for Schroeder's benefit. Greater enthusiasm there cannot be, and I tremble to think of the future, for it is scarcely possible to rise higher than this." [19]

And yet, at the premiere of *Oberon* in London on April 12, 1825, the composer "had an even more enthusiastic reception than that bestowed on Rossini two or three years before." [19]

To understand the reference to Rossini, it may help to

read of the premiere of *Tancredi* at Venice in 1813 (when Rossini, by the way, was only 21): "The work was received with enthusiasm. All Venice, and very soon all Italy, was singing or humming *mi rivedrai, ti rivedro*. One must read the accounts of the day to understand the madness—for it was nothing else—which *Tancredi* excited among the Venetians." [19]

Of *Il Barbiere* we read that it "was hissed on the first night, listened to with patience on the second, and ended by becoming one of the most popular comic operas ever composed." [19] *La Cenerentola* was "an unmistakable success," *La Gazza Ladra* a "triumph," and *Mosè* created "a profound impression." [19]

When Rossini visited Vienna in 1817, "the enthusiasm of the Viennese—like that of all to whom these fresh and animated strains (*Tancredi* and *L'Italiana in Algeri*) were brought—knew no bounds." [19] In Paris in 1823 "a serenade, a public banquet, triumphant receptions at the opera house, a special vaudeville (*Rossini à Paris, ou Le grand diner*)— everything, in short, that could soothe the pride of a stranger —was lavished upon him from the first." [19]

Of the contemporary popularity of Rossini's successors in the domination of Italian opera, Donizetti and Bellini, there is probably little reason to speak. Even music appreciation does not dispute their rapport with their audiences, although it is inclined to allude to it condescendingly as an indication that they were superficial talents. How profound this popularity was may be gathered from Rossini's description of Bellini's funeral in Paris in 1835 (he died at 34):

"The funeral took place with everyone participating, including particularly all artists, and with a pomp worthy of a king. Two hundred voices sang the Requiem, and the best artists of the capital vied with one another for the honor of singing in the chorus. . . . A brass band of 120 accompanied the procession to the cemetery . . . I can assure you that the number of people and the extent of the grief which one could discern on their faces was indescribable." [21]

Chorley wrote of *I Puritani*: "From the first to last note it was found enchanting. . . . London was steeped in the music; organs ground it, adventurous amateurs dared it, and the singers themselves sang it to such satiety as to lose all consciousness of what they were in . . ." [14]

With Verdi the matter is more complicated. Enough has been made of his being turned down at the Conservatory of Milan (for excellent reasons, it is now admitted), the failure under personally tragic circumstances of his *Un Giorno di Regno*, the initial failure of *La Traviata*, and the fact that such of his own favorites as *Macbeth* and *Simon Boccanegra* were never fully successful, to distort the case in favor of the sentimentalists. The following, excerpted from Toye's standard biography, [22] may help to restore a proper perspective:

"*Nabucco* . . . was given for the first time at La Scala on March 9, 1842, after only twelve days' rehearsal. To describe it as a brilliant success would be an understatement. *Nabucco* made Verdi the fashion. . . . Ties, hats and even sauces were named after him."

Among subsequent early operas, *I Lombardi, Ernani, I due Foscari* and *La Battaglia di Legnano* were all successful, the latter being received, according to Toye, with "delirious enthusiasm." *Ernani* was produced in fifteen theaters within nine months of the premiere.

Then came *Rigoletto*. According to a contemporary account cited by Toye, "it had the most complete success, and the composer was acclaimed, applauded and called after almost every number, two of which had to be repeated." Even Verdi, "the most restrained of men," used the extreme superlative in describing the reception to a friend a week later.[22] The article in Grove calls it "as great and deserved a success as was ever achieved by any operatic composer."

Il Trovatore followed in 1853. A contemporary account states: "The music transported us to heaven . . . The public listened to every number in religious silence and broke into applause at every interval, the end of the third act and the whole of the fourth arousing such enthusiasm that their repetition was demanded." [22]

Un ballo in maschera and *Don Carlo* were both successful and of *Aïda* the contemporary accounts "are little but chronicles of an evening of enthusiasm and triumph." [22] And then came the *Requiem*. For those who may still hold that the operas thus far mentioned are among the more superficial and conventional of Verdi's achievements, the following from Toye's account of the reception of the *Requiem* should be instructive:

"The production of the Mass had aroused European interest, and people came from France, Germany and Austria to hear it. The church could not contain anything like all those desirous of gaining admission; even such important visitors as journalists from Paris had to be accommodated in the organ loft. Wherefore three further performances (the first conducted by Verdi himself) were arranged at La Scala.

"During the performance the enthusiasm grew until the Offertorium was actually encored; so was the Sanctus. But the climax was reached in the Agnus Dei where 'the applause changed to roars which, though stifled, even broke out during the actual performance, so irresistible was the inspiration of the music.' Needless to say, this, too, was encored, and afterwards, amid the wild plaudits of the assembly, a silver crown on an elegant cushion was presented to Verdi. . . . The Mass took Italy by storm. So much so that the law had to be invoked to prevent unauthorized performances in other

Italian cities. Bologna had ventured to perform it with four pianos instead of an orchestra; Ferrara with a military band."

For the fate of *Otello*, we have again the word of Toye: "Managers and critics from all Europe were present in force. . . . What would their verdict be? As to the reception of the opera by the public there was soon no doubt. Twice in the first act, after the fire chorus and Iago's drinking song, they tried, though vainly, to call Verdi on the stage. When at the end of the act, Verdi took his call, 'one immense simultaneous shout makes the theater rock. Verdi bends his head and smiles, the frantic enthusiasm of the huge assembly bringing tears to his eyes. . . . At the end of the opera renewed and even greater enthusiasm. When the composer left the theater, a crowd of admirers, who throughout the day had lined the streets to applaud his every appearance, unharnessed the horses from his carriage and drew it to the Hotel di Milano, where he always stayed.' "

It was the same with *Falstaff*. "Needless to say," says Toye, "the performance was a brilliant success; the veneration and enthusiasm of the public for Verdi would have ensured as much in any event. The packed theater, the electric atmosphere, the calls for Verdi and the principal interpreters, the acclamation of the dense crowds in the street—were but a repetition of those already described on the occasion of *Otello*."

It is appropriate here to move back in time to include Mendelssohn. As with Donizetti and Bellini, his successes are acknowledged by music appreciation, and rather held against him. It is worth noting, however, how early his success was achieved and how deep an impression he made upon the affections of his contemporaries.

At his first appearance in England in 1829, when he was about 20, Mendelssohn introduced his *Symphony in C minor*. "The applause," says Grove, "was immense, and the *Scherzo*

was obstinately encored against his wish." Three years later
we find the Philharmonic Society passing a resolution asking
him to compose a symphony, an overture, and a vocal piece
and offering a hundred guineas for the exclusive right of
performance during two years.[19]

His "Scotch" Symphony was played in London in 1842
"amid extraordinary applause and enthusiasm." [19] And in
1846 Mendelssohn himself wrote of the premiere of *Eli-
jah*: "No work of mine ever went so admirably or was received with such enthusiasm both by musicians and the public." [19] According to Grove, "no less than four choruses and
four arias were encored. The applause at the conclusion of
both first and second parts was enormous—almost gro-
tesquely so."

During the summer of 1842 the king of Prussia conferred
upon Mendelssohn, in company with Liszt, Meyerbeer, and
Rossini, the great honor of the *Ordre pour le mérite*. At this
time Mendelssohn was still only 33. He died at 39, and of
his last illness and death at Leipzig, Grove writes:

"The public feeling was intense. Bulletins were issued, and
the house was besieged by inquirers. After his death it was
as if everyone in the town had received a blow and sustained
a personal loss."

Mendelssohn's contemporary, Schumann, admittedly had
harder going. To this his wife's fame and his own reticence
certainly contributed. But here also the record does not support the superstition of contemporary neglect. Wallace
Brockway and Herbert Weinstock, in their *Men of Music*,[23] recall that Schumann himself wrote, following the
premiere of his "Spring" Symphony in Leipzig in 1841, that
it had been "received as no other (symphony) since Beethoven." And Paul Henry Lang states: "In 1846 Clara presented his Piano Concerto amid jubilation, and none of the
ensuing years was without resounding success . . ." [4]

An extraordinary career was being made during these same years by Meyerbeer, whose operas held the stage for a full century. That they have now disappeared from the stage is a fact of which those who speak glibly of the "verdict of posterity" should occasionally be reminded. His *Crociato* in 1824 "created a furore, the composer being called for and crowned on the stage." [19] Then came *Robert le diable* in 1831, "of which the unparalleled success extended in a very few years over the whole civilized world." [19] *Les Huguenots* started less spectacularly, but "the public was soon forced to acknowledge the incontrovertible truth that it was immeasurably the superior of the two." [19]

From Meyerbeer it is but a chronological step to Berlioz, one of the oddest cases of all. So much has been made of Berlioz's difficulties in Paris and the failure of some of his fondest projects (all of which have remained failures to this day), that his several remarkable Parisian successes have been passed over and his unexampled triumphs abroad overlooked entirely.

One of the most extraordinary successes in musical history was that of the premiere of the *Symphonie fantastique* and the cantata *Sardanapolis* in Paris in 1830, when the composer was only 20 years old. For a description of this reception we have Berlioz's own account: [15]

"The performance was by no means perfect, as two rehearsals are wholly insufficient for such complicated works; but they went well enough for their principal features to be appreciated. *Le bal, La marche* and *Le sabbat* created a great sensation; The March especially carried the audience by storm . . . The cantata was well performed; the conflagration took place, the great crash followed, and the success was immense."

Nor was this all, even in Paris. *Harold in Italy* was, "even in its first form, always successful." [15] At the premiere of the *Carnaval Romain* the public cried "*Bis*," and "we played the overture over again." [15] And of *Romeo et Juliette* Berlioz wrote: "The work, such as it was then, was performed three times at the Conservatoire under my own direction, apparently with great success."

Berlioz's fame and acceptance abroad were astounding. He traveled to Germany, Austria, Hungary, Russia, and England, introducing his own works and scoring successes unparalleled by any other composer of instrumental music in his generation, and this despite the fact that he was offering works of a decidedly revolutionary cast with orchestras to whom they were utterly unfamiliar. One can imagine how far the performances were from what one hears today.

These successes are summed up in Grove: "The tour (of Germany in 1843) was a triumphant success. . . . He was received everywhere with crowded audiences and enthusiastic applause. . . . The whole campaign was one long triumphal procession. He returned covered with laurels. In 1845 he made an equally successful tour in Austria. . . . Next year he won fresh triumphs in Russia."

What these triumphs looked like in detail is recorded for us in Berlioz's own words. His description of the concert in Brunswick in 1843 is an example:

"The overture was received with great acclamation, the *Pilgrims' March* was encored, the *Orgie* put the whole room in a fever, the devout were evidently deeply moved by the *Offertoire* and the *Quaerens me . . . Queen Mab* created a sensation; a song with orchestra was encored, and the *Feast at the Capulets* formed a glowing finale to the evening.

"Scarcely had the last chord been struck when a terrible noise shook the entire room, the whole public *en masse* hallooing (from pit, boxes—everywhere); the trumpets, horns and trombones of the orchestra, some in one key and some in another, made the most discordant fanfares, accompanied by all the fracas that it was possible to make with bows on the backs of violins and basses, and with the percussion. . . . It was impossible not to be moved by their homage when the Kapellmeister came forward laden with flowers, and said in French, 'Permit me, sir, to offer you these wreaths in the name of the ducal band, and allow me to lay them on your scores.' At these words the public redoubled its applause, the orchestra recommenced its fanfares. . . . the baton fell from my hand, and I was no longer aware of what was going on." [15]

Another of the great innovators was Chopin. He was accepted from the very start. At the concert given prior to his departure from Warsaw, when he was only 20, and which included the Concerto in F minor, "the interest taken in him was so great that every seat was occupied and a second and even a third concert had to be given." [19]

When he played this same concerto in Paris two years later, according to Casimir Wierzynski in his *Life and Death of Chopin*, [24] "The audience was equally amazed and delighted by it. . . . Chopin became the fashion in Paris. He had many pupils and charged twenty francs an hour. The struggling Bohemian had become a celebrity." Chopin himself wrote: "I have entered the highest society. I sit among ambassadors, princes, ministers. . . ." [24]

According to Wierzynski, "Chopin was adding ever greater luster to his name. Revolutionary as his ideas were, he not only vindicated his innovations but also won increasing popularity. His works were performed by Kalkbrenner, Liszt, Hiller, Osborne, Stamaty, Clara Wieck, and Edward Wolff. Painters were eager to make portraits of him; sculptors modeled his exquisite profile in relief, and in Poland etchings of his face sold at ten zlotys apiece."

When he played the E minor Concerto in Rouen in 1838, the critic Ernest Legouve wrote: "Through this time one could feel that the hall was electrified and hear the murmur of rapture and amazement that may be considered the unconscious utterance of souls carried away by enthusiasm!" [24]

Liszt wrote of his concert in Paris on 26 April, 1841 in the *Gazette Musicale*: "One paean of praise was on the lips of all." And of a concert in February, 1848, the same periodical reported: "What a success, what enthusiasm! It is easier to tell you what a welcome he was accorded, what raptures he aroused, etc." [24]

The case of Wagner calls for special attention. He had many difficulties, and much has been made of them, but they were due rather to his own stubbornness in refusing to tailor his works to the requirements and facilities of theaters than to any lack of popular enthusiasm. He was entitled to his stubbornness, but he had little right to be indignant at what it cost him. In view of the fact that the Vienna Opera, for instance, gave *Tristan und Isolde* seventy-some rehearsals before abandoning it, he could hardly complain of lack of recognition and good will. Certainly he could not complain of lack of public interest.

Heinrich Heine attended the premiere of *Rienzi* in 1842 and reported that "The Dresdeners were no longer Dresdeners. . . . In one place all the note gourmandizers and counterpoint-cocks laid their heads together and declared openly that with this opera Wagner had placed himself in line with the worthiest masters; in another loathsome Italianised fools . . . who peck like sparrows at Beethoven, Mozart, Weber, and Marschner, were of the opinion that the work 'surpassed even the divine Donizetti.'" The applause, said Heine, "had been terrific." [25]

Tannhäuser got off to an uncertain start in 1843, but as Ernest Newman has recounted, "A fourth performance before a packed house followed . . . and thereafter '*Tann-*

häuser' proved a steady draw . . . (Wagner) saw, with great gratification, that it appealed particularly to the more cultured and thoughtful section of the public, and that this section grew steadily in numbers." [25]

At about this time a young critic named Eduard Hanslick, in Vienna, having heard a performance of *Tannhäuser* in Dresden, wrote: "Richard Wagner is, I am convinced, the greatest dramatic talent among all contemporary composers." [26]

Ten years later, this same Hanslick, while moving over to the opposition, said of *Lohengrin* in Vienna: "The success which Richard Wagner's *Lohengrin* enjoyed here . . . was so brilliant that certain observations . . . may not be amiss. . . . The verdict of the public as a whole has been impressively unanimous. It is a fact that persons of the most divers sorts and conditions . . . have seen *Lohengrin* half a dozen times and enjoyed it." [26]

When the Bayreuth project was launched, Grove notes: "It appeared at once that all over Germany there were numbers of people who were ready to contribute their share of work and money. . . . Societies sprang up on all sides—not only in Germany, but in the most unexpected quarters—St. Petersburg, Warsaw, New York, Amsterdam, Brussels, Paris, Stockholm, Cairo, Milan, London, etc."

Of the success of the project, of *Der Ring des Nibelungen* and the subsequent *Parsifal,* there is no need to speak. When Wagner died in 1883, Hanslick could write:

"Wagner died a happy man. It was recently his privilege to bring his last great work to life in Bayreuth, to rejoice in its actual preparation, and to bask in the sunlight of such success as no other artist of any time or nation has enjoyed." [26]

On Wagner's contemporary, Brahms, the record is in less dispute. As Grove puts it: "From that time (1853) until

the master's death, every new composition of his was the subject of immediate discussion. Happier circumstances it would
be difficult to imagine for the creative artist."

Hanslick's reviews of the symphonies offer a chronological
record of the greater successes. Of the Symphony No. 1:
"Seldom, if ever, has the musical world awaited a composer's
first symphony with such intense anticipation." Of the Symphony No. 2, "The novelty was a great, unqualified success."
Of the Symphony No. 3, "(It) is a feast for the music lover
and musician rather than for the critic." And of the Symphony No. 4: "Since its first performance in Meiningen this
symphony has enjoyed a series of triumphs. Everyone who
had read the enthusiastic reports from Frankfurt, Cologne
and Elberfeld, and even those who had not, expected something great and unique." [26]

Dvorak enjoyed a similar history. Grove speaks of Dvorak's
own performance of his Symophony in D and other works at
the Philharmonic Society concerts in London, "invariably
meeting with the enthusiastic ovations from the public and
those who took part in the music." In 1892 he was given an
honorary Ph.D. from the Czech University in Prague, was
elected to the Czech Academy of Art and Science and awarded
the Order of the Iron Crown from Emperor Franz Josef I. In
1892 he migrated to America, "where he met with a splendid reception." [19]

Of Tchaikovsky we read: [19] "At the concert on October
28, the *Symphonie Pathétique* fell rather flat. A few weeks
later it made a profound sensation." The *Nutcracker Suite*
was received, at its premiere, "with immense enthusiasm,
five of the six movements having to be repeated." [19]
During his American tour in 1891, Tchaikovsky "met with
unprecedented success," and the press notices were written in
a tone of "unqualified praise." [19] The skeptical Hanslick re-

corded a "lively success" for the *Symphonie Pathétique* in Vienna, a success "profound enough to pave the way in Vienna for other compositions of this prolific composer." [26]

Even Bruckner had his earthly rewards. Of the premiere of his Eighth Symphony in Vienna, we have again the word of Hanslick, who was certainly not prejudiced in the composer's favor: "And the reception of the new symphony? A stormy ovation, waving of handkerchiefs from the standees, innumerable recalls, laurel wreaths, etc. For Bruckner the concert was certainly a huge success." [26]

As Ernest Newman has said, "We have been inclined to regard Mendelssohn as Fortune's Favorite among musicians; but she was even kinder to Strauss. . . . In 1903, when the Sinfonia Domestica was produced, he was not yet forty, but already he was accepted everywhere as the foremost living composer. . . . I am afraid he would have been the last to accept Mr. Slonimsky's dogma of the 'Non-Acceptance of the Unfamiliar' in music; his own works were exceptionally daring for their day, yet in spite of what several of the critics said about them, they swept the board."

To complete the account of the symphonists, there is the case of Sibelius. According to Grove: "In little more than three years after his return home . . . he won such recognition that a life grant was offered him by the state in 1897, on which he was able to retire and to devote himself entirely to a creative career. . . . Both his fiftieth and sixtieth birthdays were celebrated in Helsingfors as events of national importance." Needless to add, his subsequent birthdays were similarly celebrated.

The record of the opera composers is no less impressive, but it can be dealt with briefly. *Faust* "placed Gounod at once in the first rank of living composers." [19] *La Juive* was "a sensational success." [28] Saint-Saëns' career, "from the middle 'sixties onward . . . was one of almost uninterrupted success." [19] Massenet was appointed professor of advanced composition at the *Conservatoire* and elected a member of the *Académie des Beaux Arts* in 1878 when he was only 36, the youngest member to be so honored (and six years before the appearance of *Manon*).[19] Offenbach's *The Tales of Hoffman* was played no fewer than 101 times in the year following its production.[19] *Hänsel und Gretel* "triumphed just as completely in Vienna as it had triumphed previously in the major musical centers of Germany." [26] Charpentier's *Louise* was a "remarkable success." [29] *Andrea Chenier* was "a decided success, which soon established itself in the international repertoire." [29]

Manon Lescaut was greeted "with ovations," [30] and with *La Bohème* Puccini "surpassed all his previous triumphs." [19] *Cavalleria Rusticana* was received at its first performance "with tumultuous applause, and the next day Mascagni awoke to find himself famous. Everywhere its success was unquestionable." [19] The premiere of *Pagliacci* in 1892 was "a very great success, and Leoncavallo's name soon became famous throughout Italy." [19] Even *Pelléas et Mélisande,* "irrespective of widely diverging critical opinions, was an unexpected success, with many repetitions of the work now ensuing. Debussy, now famous, was tendered (and accepted) a government decoration." [29]

Such, then, is the record of Non-Acceptance of the Unfamiliar. It must be emphasized that this record includes all the most daring, rebellious, revolutionary, and radical innovators of the nineteenth century, among them Beethoven, Berlioz, Chopin, Verdi, Wagner, and Strauss. And it should be emphasized again that this is a record of popular rather than critical approbation.

Shortly after the turn of the century the picture changes. The audience begins to rebel, vociferously at first, then by the expression of boredom and indifference. There have been few really popular successes since the First World War, and most of them have belonged to the novelty category.

To compare the picture of the relationship between composer and public in the eighteenth and nineteenth centuries which this record discloses with the relationship existing today is both fascinating and instructive. Can one imagine twelve policemen and eighteen mounted guards being required to clear the sidewalks at the premiere of an oratorio by Honegger or Stravinsky? Is it possible that any critic could write of anything written in the past 50 years, "Three days have gone by since that enrapturing evening"?

Did anyone suppose that Schönberg's funeral procession would be accompanied by a brass band of 120, or that singers like Helen Traubel, Leonard Warren, Richard Tucker, and Robert Merrill would be fighting for the privilege of singing in the chorus at a cantata in his memory? Can one conceive of singers singing the melodies of Frank Martin's *Le Vin Herbé* to "such satiety as to lose all consciousness of what they were in"? Or of Salzburg and Vienna being swept by madness by the tunes of Von Einem's *Der Prozess*?

Can one imagine any contemporary composer becoming the fashion? Will one find a "Steak Honegger" in Paris, a "Blacher Torte" in Berlin, or a "Suppe Jelinek" in Vienna? Is it conceivable that "adventurous amateurs" might dare *Lady Macbeth of Mzensk,* or that a deliriously enthusiastic audience might demand a repetition of the last act of *Wozzeck?* Or that the policeman's band of any city in the United States or Europe might get into trouble for pirating *The Rake's Progress* or *Peter Grimes?* Or etchings of any contemporary American composer selling for 50 cents apiece on the streets of New York?

These are all silly questions. The fact that they are so very silly is the most conclusive proof of the distance by which composers and the public are now separated. Only one composer since the First World War has achieved such popularity, has been so admired, applauded, and loved. That was George Gershwin. And he alone of all the composers mentioned thus far was identified primarily with American popular music. He originated as a popular composer, grew up as a popular composer, and died a popular composer.

A certain naive humility before the intellectual aura of "serious" music, and an awareness of technical limitations, caused him to underestimate his own gifts and to overestimate the quality of the gifts of composers like Stravinsky, Ravel, and Schönberg. Thus he aspired to write "serious" music. Of his actual excursions in the "serious" field it would probably be most accurate to say that his talent was big enough to survive them. Certainly there is nothing in the *Rhapsody in Blue* or *An American in Paris* to compare in simple, spontaneous creative genius with *The Man I Love* or *Embraceable You.*

In all of musical history there is probably no more touching evidence of an upside down state of cultural affairs than the spectacle of George Gershwin going to Schönberg for composition lessons. Schönberg is reported to have suggested, in view of their relative earning power, that the roles should be reversed. Probably the suggestion was more rueful than sincere.

Be that as it may, the contemporary composer's position outside society is, as we have seen, not a normal one. His argument that this is the way it has always been is a rationalization without foundation in fact.

2

THE COMPOSER

AND

HIS MATERIALS

THE CRISIS OF EVOLUTION I

⋄⋄⋄

THAT the art of music has, for the past fifty years, been experiencing a period of evolutionary crisis is accepted by composers, critics, and everyone else seriously concerned. The area of general agreement extends even to common recognition of the gap between composer and audience and to the identification of tonal harmony as the decisive point of technical exhaustion and breakdown.

If there is general agreement about the existence of a crisis, however, and a good deal of unanimity in the diagnosis, there is no similar consensus in the appraisal of its significance, or in the recommendations of means to achieve its resolution.

The twelve-tonists feel that the answer to the crisis of harmony is a systematized atonality. Schönberg, Berg, Webern, and many others whose names are less familiar to laymen, have taken this conclusion as a point of departure. They assume, not without some logic, that a musical art that has been growing less and less tonal for more than a century of evolution must certainly have an atonal destination. If this is the direction in which music has been headed for so long, they argue, then it must also be the direction in which it is fated to continue.

Others, headed originally by Stravinsky, believe that a

fusion of modern technique with classical forms and concepts affords an opportunity for further progress. The neo-classical composers have no difficulty persuading themselves that this is neither reactionary in conception nor retrogressive in practice. As Stravinsky put it in his *Poetics of Music*: [31] "The true tradition is not the symbol of a forgotten past; it is a living force that inspires and instructs the present. . . . One associates oneself with a tradition in order to create something new."

Indeed, the neo-classicists can even persuade themselves that they are really revolutionaries and, by implication, progressives. The return to classical models, as they see it, represents a revolt against the formal license and emotional excesses of the late nineteenth century, while the employment of modern harmony and modern instrumentation is a guarantee against the charge of antiquarianism or reaction that might otherwise result from such a demonstrated preference for a better-ordered past.

In neither case, atonal nor neo-classic, has the result contributed to a lessening of the gap between composer and public. The lay listener is as little charmed by one as by the other. While the composer works out his esthetic and technical problems on the basis of analyses and deductions, however mistaken, and by methods however repulsive, the problem of music and the public goes by default.

The history of music in any civilization, including our own, is the history of music that people like. Music is unthinkable without an audience. It has no existence without listeners. Its history is determined, not by composers and critics, but by lay listeners. True, it is the composer, not the listener, who produces new ideas. This is why great innovators among the composers, such as Beethoven, Berlioz, and Wagner, are thought of as influencing and even determining the course of musical history. But this overlooks the fact that their new ideas are valid only insofar as they are acceptable to the listening public. Thus, in the wider sense it is the public that determines the course of evolution by rendering its verdict as to which among any number of new ideas it finds to its taste.

All the previous crises in the history of Western music have been crises of composer-audience relations. They have not necessarily always found all the composers lined up on one side and all the listeners on the other. Listeners and composers have often been somewhat divided among themselves. But essentially every crisis has revolved around a conflict between complexity and simplicity, with the composers, particularly the established composers, lined up on the side of complexity, and the listeners, possibly inspired by younger composers of radical disposition, lined up on the side of simplicity. Indeed, the history of Western music betrays certain pendulum-like characteristics in the various shifts from simplicity to complexity, from complexity to simplicity.

Generally speaking, the move from simplicity to complexity has proceeded under the banner of progress. Such moves are recorded in the development of modal polyphony from the fourteenth to the sixteenth centuries, in the development of German tonal polyphony which ended with Bach, and in the whole romantic chapter usually thought of as beginning with Beethoven and culminating in Wagner.

The trend in the opposite direction, from complexity to simplicity, has commonly been hailed as a healthy return to musical grass roots, as a kind of intellectual and esthetic sobering up. Examples of this kind of reaction have been the monodic Italian opera at the beginning of the seventeenth century, the opera reforms of Gluck, Mozart, and Cimarosa in the eighteenth, and the Italian verismo operas and a *Pelléas et Mélisande* at the turn of the nineteenth.

The metaphor of the pendulum is weakened only by the

fact that the move from simplicity to complexity has always been gradual, and extended over a long period of time, while the move from complexity to simplicity has usually been drastic and rapid, prompted by a popular rebellion against a kind of music in which complexity ceased to be fascinating to the layman and tended to make music the exclusive property of professionals and initiates. After such a rebellion the move toward complexity sets in again, from a new starting point in simplicity.

Looking at it in another way, we see the listener over a number of generations fascinated by musical evolution, awed and charmed by new, fresh, and ingenious marvels of complexity, sharing vicariously the composer's pride of achievement as he conquers one obstacle after another, and even participating, in a sense, as arbiter of what is admissible and what is not.

At a certain point, however, the composer becomes so preoccupied with his complex problems of structure and syntax as to confuse ends and means and to forget music's popular purpose. The listener finds that he can no longer either follow or enjoy the composer's problems—and the game is over. Then ensues a hiatus during which the listener looks to the past for his musical pleasure, and the composer looks to the future for an audience.

Honegger has touched briefly but articulately on this as it applies to the present. "It is always a question," he says, "of supply and demand. Nowadays fewer and fewer people are buying scores. There are several reasons for this. First the reading of modern scores has become very difficult, and these difficulties frighten even the type of layman who used to make a hobby of deciphering scores at the piano. Fifty years ago you could find *Carmen*, *Faust*, *Manon* and *Werther* in every bourgeois home that had a piano. Since *Pelléas* one asks simply why composers write such esoteric, unintelligible stuff." [1] *

Hindemith puts it as follows: "Our modern music, compared with the music of earlier times, has reached a very high level of complexity. An individual composer, aware of this fact, usually wants to contribute his share to this presumed progress of music, and thereupon he adds complications of his own—complications of technique which will eventually fracture the framework set up by the physical and mental conditions of musical performance and complications of style which in their ultimate esoteric loneliness are bound to reach the borderline of unintelligible enigmas." [2]

Krenek has approached the problem from the point of view of the twelve-tonists and comes up with the following:

"Since the pattern of development in individual artists as well as in the larger sense of general styles usually betrays a trend from simplicity, we are tempted to assume that complexity as opposed to simplicity signifies progress. Atonality, as inaugurated by Schönberg, ranks among the most complicated phenomena in the history of music.

"In view of analogous historical situations, we should hardly be surprised to find again today a tendency toward simplicity. For about twenty years music has been undergoing a reaction against the complexity of atonality and the twelve-tone technique. This reaction is distinguished from similar processes in the past primarily by the fact that it was not introduced by a new generation of composers but rather by the leading composers of an established generation, almost all of whom began complexly and moved toward simplicity. Bartok, Milhaud, Hindemith, and Stravinsky may be cited as examples.

* *Je suis compositeur,* by Arthur Honegger. Copyright by Editions du Conquistador, Paris, 1951.

"The new simplicity as revealed by both older and younger composers is distinct from similar movements in the past in that it is not restricted to the simplification of structure but reaches back to a previous musical language, namely tonality. The post-Bach primitives cannot be cited as parallels, since the musical language was not changed. It was tonal both before and after. A hypothetical parallel would have the composers of the seventeenth century, confused by Monteverdi's innovations, going back to the modal style of Palestrina. It is just this effort to recall past circumstances that gives the new simplicity its fatal reactionary flavor." [13]

This is a remarkably instructive statement, distinguished not only by critical insight, but also by an uncommonly acute historical perspective. Krenek is certainly correct in his observation of a reaction in favor of simplicity on the part of many composers who began complexly. He is also correct, as far as the neo-classicists are concerned, in noting that this reaction looks to tonality for its salvation. Most astute of all is his recognition of the present crisis as something more profound and far-reaching than any of the various shifts in the trends of composition and popular taste represented by such non-conformists as Gluck, Mozart, Beethoven, Berlioz, Wagner, and Debussy. In these previous crises, as Krenek notes, "The language was not changed. It was tonal both before and after." That what is now involved in atonality or the twelve-tone system, is, indeed, a change of language is the single most important factor to be remembered in any attempt to appraise the situation and condition of contemporary serious music.

It is all very well to say that atonality has been prepared by a long period of tonal disintegration. But this does not mean that the change from a tonal to an atonal musical language would not be drastic. As long as there is a shred of tonal feeling left among music lovers, and a shred of tonal resource left unexploited by composers, the frame of musical reference is still tonal. But once an atonal frame of reference were generally accepted, then music would have stepped across a linguistic border, however short the step. As Krenek has put it elsewhere, "We must go back to Monteverdi's time in order to observe a transition from one tonal language to another corresponding to that which took place with Schönberg." [13]

The transition to which Krenek refers in citing Monteverdi is, of course, the transition from modal polyphony to tonal harmony. This is the transition separating the two great distinctive periods of Western music, i.e., the modal epoch and the harmonic epoch. None of the many changes that occurred in the course of either of these epochs could compare in significance with the great cataclysm at the end of the sixteenth century when the modes gave way before the diatonic scale and opened the way to the tonal, or harmonic epoch. It is the latter epoch that has produced the whole literature familiar to us as classical or serious music.

Today's music lover may listen to and even derive pleasure from the contrapuntal masterpieces of the polyphonic epoch, but he cannot hear them as they were heard in their own time, since he brings to their hearing certain habits of listening derived from his exclusive association with tonal rather than modal music. He cannot accept a modal term of reference. As in listening to oriental music, he is impressed, not by what impresses its own listeners, but by the manner in which it represents a deviation from the music to which he is accustomed. He is like a Berliner listening to the Dutch language or an Alpine Germanic dialect.

This explains Krenek's device in comparing the neo-classical composers with hypothetical composers of the seventeenth century, "confused by Monteverdi's innovations, going back to the modal style of Palestrina." What he is saying is that atonality is to tonality what tonality was to modality, or tonal harmony to modal polyphony. The neo-classicists, he tells us, do not recognize the new atonal language, or at least do not feel at home in it, and seek refuge in the old language of tonality.

It is probably the most perceptive and articulate definition of the real meaning of neo-classicism that has ever been made, and Krenek's reference to its "fatal reactionary flavor" can hardly be regarded either as impertinent or overdrawn. Its pertinence is confirmed by the neo-classicists themselves. Theodore Stravinsky, the composer's son, has unwittingly given the play away in his analysis of his father's neo-classicism, an analysis, by the way, that enjoys his father's written endorsement. He says, for instance, in *Le message d'Igor Strawinsky*: [32]

"When Stravinsky 'looks back' or 'returns' to something, then it is to a great fundamental dogma which in the course of an entire romantic century has been almost completely forgotten—to pure music, to music as an absolute art . . . But if his musical credo embraces the oldest tradition, still it does so with the essential difference that that which with the old masters was spontaneous (and doubtless usually unconscious) is with Stravinsky fully conscious, considered, and reasoned. . . . Whether one finds this a reason for rejoicing or lamentation, this is today a firm fact that can no longer be denied or evaded. . . . This conscious awareness is one of the most significant factors in the musical history of our culture."

And it explains why so many of these composers have never achieved in their reasoned effort to achieve simplicity anything like the quality and the popularity attained in their earlier works, written more complexly but also more spontaneously. Of this, Stravinsky, Ravel, and Richard Strauss are prime examples.

Krenek touches on this when he notes that "this reaction is distinguished from similar processes in the past primarily by the fact that it was not introduced by a new generation of composers but rather by the leading composers of an established generation." He might better have noted that it was not, indeed, a popular reaction, but rather a tactical reversal of the field by composers whose relation with the public had already become tenuous and whose intellectual instincts and predilections prompted them to look backward instead of around them. Confronted by what Honegger has called "a wall of accumulated materials," [1] they turned tail.

But the over-all validity of Krenek's argument depends upon whether or not atonality is, indeed, a new musical language. That it is intended as a new language need not be questioned, nor the assumption that, if it is a language, it is a new one. The basic questions remain: Is atonality a musical language? If it is a language, has it any other than an academic future?

The answer to the first question is that atonality is probably a language in the sense that those who devised it also employ it, and even seem to understand it. It is also a language in the sense that it is recognized as such even by composers who do not employ it. If musical evolution is in the hands of the composers, then the linguistic crisis is real.

The answer to the second question, however, whether it has any future, is a different matter. Real languages are not made. They evolve from the compulsion of people to communicate with one another, and their characteristics are determined by the circumstances of the communities in which they evolve. Scholars may codify them and set general standards of vocabulary, grammar, and syntax, but they cannot invent them. At least, they cannot make an invented language stick. Of this Esperanto is a pertinent present example.

Krenek may correctly note the "fatal reactionary flavor" of neo-classical music, but as a twelve-tonist he overlooks the fatal academic flavor of a new musical language without popular roots. The final test of a language is: Do people use it? Applied to music this test emerges: Is it a people's music? Exposed to this test, atonality collapses.

In other words, the interpretation of the present crisis of musical evolution as a linguistic crisis is valid only to those who think of evolution as the exclusive responsibility of serious composers. If this were the case, then one would have to acknowledge the atonalists as the standard-bearers of progress. But the absence of popular origins in their new musical language, and the inability and disinclination of the musical community to adopt it, indicate conclusively that this is not the path of musical evolution and that atonality is, in fact, a still-born language.

The only serious composer who has combined insight with the courage to face the facts and draw the consequences is the German Carl Orff. He has recognized the obsolescence both of the harmonic system and of the symphony orchestra as well as the obsolescence of the classical forms, and has thrown the whole apparatus overboard, reverting to the simplest melodic, rhythmic, and harmonic formulas. The re-action of his contemporaries, both composers and critics, has been to regard him as a non-musician. In a sense they are right. It is a matter of definition. If one finds Berg, Webern, Hindemith, etc., musical, then it is certainly consistent to find that Orff is no musician.

But even Orff cannot escape sociology. His compositions may reveal a more profound critical and historical under-standing of the contemporary musical situation than the music of his contemporaries. His impulse to get back to the basic elements of melody and rhythm is certainly correct. But his compositions, like those of his contemporaries, also represent a critical rather than a spontaneously popular creative accomplishment.

Such works as *Antigone* and even the more easily assimilable *Trionfi,* are admirable in their avoidance of the technical delusions that beset every other contemporary composer, and delightful in the drastic manner in which they defy the instrumental and harmonic conventions hitherto accepted as indispensable to serious music. But they have no popular roots.

Even Orff is inhibited by the assumption of the inevitability of an art music separate and distinct from popular music. He has seen his colleagues stumped by the "wall of accumulated materials" and has understood the futility of their exploratory enterprises. He has recognized the necessity for radical measures. And he has done the only thing that he, as a serious composer, could do. He has gone back to primitive elements, to the Middle Ages, to the Greeks, and to Africa and the Orient.

This is preferable to the compromise retreat of the neoclassicists to the eighteenth century, or to the esoteric adventures of the twelve-tonists in atonality, but it collapses in the face of the sheer fact that the crisis of evolution is not susceptible of intellectual solution. The problem is not to find a new system. It is to find the audience.

The neo-classicist, at least, offers the old audience something related to what it has previously heard, however inferior. The listener finds himself on fairly solid ground, if surrounded by a forbidding landscape. The atonalist, on the other hand, provides him with no point of reference, even within the framework of a single composition, since repetition is a heresy in the dogma of atonalism. And an Orff, except in the relatively popular *Carmina Burana*, gives only an intellectually distilled primitiveness with which the audience has nothing in common.

Whatever the method, the composer's claim to historical continuity is supportable only on paper. The listener does not feel his music as music. As long as this is the case, its claim to being music at all is dubious. It has been the case now for nearly fifty years. This would have to be reckoned a long time in any period of history. It is a particularly long time in such a period as our own, when evolution in every phase of life has been so accelerated.

It is a long enough time, indeed, to establish as a historical fact that the composer of modern music has no audience. It remains simply for history to record that a composer without an audience, as far as evolution is concerned, is not a composer.

THE CRISIS OF HARMONY

AT SOME point in its constitutional organization the European musical system broke down. That it did, indeed, break down is conceded by almost every serious student of music. And almost every student, including particularly the composers of modern music, agrees that the point of collapse was harmony. As Hindemith has put it:

"The core of all the problems puzzling the composer . . . is the theoretical considerations concerning the nature and technical potentialities of the chordal and tonal progressions which are his material of construction." [2]

This is the fact upon which the whole technical appreciation of modern music turns. For we are concerned here not with the possibly infinite durability of the human ear, but with the demonstrably finite harmonic resources of the chromatic scale. What is involved is simply the capability of the twelve tones available to us to yield up any new harmonies.

This is a technical question of the utmost simplicity and the utmost importance. For harmony is Western music's uniquely distinguishing element.

It is polyphonic, or multiple-voiced, music that sets Western music off from the music of other civilizations. And it is the concept of tonality, or key, that sets off the harmonic era of Western music from which our standard repertoire is drawn—that is, the European art music literature extending roughly from 1600 to the present time.

The sensations communicated to the listener by progressions of chords, and the structural potentialities deriving from chordal movement are what make European music seem to mean something. They are the resources by which those points of tension, suspense, climax, release, resolution, and repose are plotted, which give music dramatic or picturesque character, content, and coherence. They are the structural materials of the architectural eloquence which everyone recognizes as the crowning glory of European music and which no one has every satisfactorily defined. To quote Sir George Dyson in his excellent article on tonality in Grove's Dictionary:

"Tonality is that element of key-feeling which was gradually evolved out of the increasingly harmonic organization of modal polyphony. In the end it completely supplanted the less universal values which had depended on the particular character of a particular mode. Throughout the whole development of classical forms key-definition has occupied a paramount place. Without it neither the harmonies nor the architecture of the music of the last three centuries can be made intelligible. Tonality in general rests mainly on a balance of tonal harmonies rendered stable and convincing by the use of a context of such related or leading chords as appear to find their ultimate solution in the desired key . . .

"Those extended forms of the sonata order on which classical instrumental music has been mainly built have acknowledged an unqualified allegiance to rigid tonalities. And this is almost equally true of every musical form which has an intrinsic architectural coherence. Keys and their relations are, in this sense, postulates on which melodic, harmonic, and formal arguments were alike founded. It was by an unfailing sensitiveness to these values that composers were able to display a wealth of imaginative fancy and yet preserve a formal balance and coherence that made an extended movement an artistically proportioned whole. It must be admitted, however, that three centuries of development have not left these fundamental conceptions of tonality altogether unqualified."

Modern composers see it in much the same way, although it is doubtful that even so reticent an individual as Webern would have been capable of the understatement of Sir George's last sentence. Schönberg has said: "Music depends not only on acoustics but upon logic and upon those particular laws which result from the combination of tone and tune. Tonality, tending to render harmonic facts perceptible and correlate them, is therefore not an end but a means." [29] Krenek has finished the thought by adding: "If tonality is a means, then what is its end? Obviously a general organization of musical material in such a way that musical structures may be comprehended as logically coherent wholes." [33] And Hindemith, observing the phenomenon of harmony in a wider historical and geographical perspective, concludes:

"There was in musical history a time when these effects of perspective—or of tonality, as the technical term goes—were unknown to musicians. This was at a time before harmonies were used consciously and when music consisted only of melodic lines. Even nowadays in many countries and cultures that are not under the domination of Western musical techniques and habits, harmony is either unknown or flatly rejected as an unwelcome addition to the native material of music, and people with this exclusively melodic conception of music cannot have any effect of the sounding perspective of tonality as expressed by harmonic reference to tonal fundamentals. With harmony it seems to go as with the tree of the knowledge of good and evil; once you have tasted its fruits you have lost your innocent approach to the facts of life. For us, after our musical development has gone through about a thousand years of musical knowledge that consisted exclusively of harmonized musical structures, it is quite impossible to understand melodic lines without harmonic and tonal implications." [2]

Thus it is not surprising that the history of Western music for the past three hundred and fifty years is largely the history of its harmony. This is the story of how composers and audiences became used to one set of harmonic conventions and were first shocked, then fascinated, and finally enchanted by a new set, sharper, bolder, more forceful, more picturesque, and apparently more eloquent. Everything else has been incidental—form, style, substance, and even instrumentation. Or, to put it more accurately, everything else has either originated in harmony or found fulfillment in harmony.

In the study of no other element of music is it so easy to trace the patterns of rise and fall, of growth and decay, of organization and disintegration. One can begin with the often crude harmonies of the seventeenth century Italians and see how later masters selected and discarded in order to arrive at the conventions governing the music of Bach, Handel, Mozart, and Haydn. One can follow the relaxation of these conventions in the music of the nineteenth century masters. One sees the trend from anarchy to order culminating in Bach, Haydn, and Mozart. And one sees the subsequent trend from order to anarchy, culminating in Wagner and Strauss.

One of the critical oddities of the times is the habit of noting how "modern" were the harmonies of such older masters as Monteverdi, Gesualdo, Gabrieli, etc., as if these men had been somehow so far ahead of their time as to anticipate ours—and as if it were suddenly becoming apparent to us now that possibly they knew more about harmony than Bach, Haydn, and Mozart did. The dissonances they employed, often similar to dissonances used today, are cited in support of the familiar argument that dissonance is simply a matter of what one generation is accustomed to regard as such.

The argumentation is irrelevant. The seventeenth century masters were experimenting in a period of evolution headed toward *perfection*. The creative processes were directed at integration, codification, organization, and refinement. The experiments of the twentieth century moderns have no such prospects of an orderly destination, least of all in harmony; for the creative processes of which they are a part are harmonically disintegrative and destructive, and have been so for a hundred and fifty years. If one is reminded, in listening to Monteverdi or Gesualdo, of modern harmonies, it is well to remember that landmarks passed on the journey up a mountain are also encountered on the journey down.

The essential point, contrary to popular belief, is that dissonance has not changed. The only change has been in the treatment of dissonance. What was dissonant in Monteverdi's time was also dissonant in Mozart's time and Wagner's, and is still dissonant in our own. In all cases dissonance is felt as a tonal clash.

The difference between dissonance then and dissonance now is that in Monteverdi, as also in Mozart and even in Wagner, the listener is excited by the clash, and quieted and rewarded by its resolution in what the listener feels to be a consonance. In modern music there is no resolution. As Stravinsky has put it, the developments of the last century have led to a point where "dissonance is no longer a symbol of disorder, nor consonance a guarantee of security." [34]

The feeling for key, or tonality, which gives each of the contending voices in a Monteverdi or Mozart dissonance a sheltered destination in a tonally agreeable consonance, is gone. Without harmonic order there are no tonal safe havens. Both composer and listener are left as hapless flotsam on a sea of tonal discomfort.

Music in which dissonance offers no prospect of resolution deprives the listener of his tonal bearings, and its claim to tonality is either academic or fraudulent. There can, of course, be music without chordal harmony. As Hindemith observes, this is the case with the music of other civilizations; but it is music which exists outside the esthetic terms of reference of Western music.

There can be tonality without chordal harmony. An unaccompanied melody can be tonal, and almost always is. The modality which governed the composition of melodies from the Greek modes was synonymous with tonality in the sense that the notes of the mode were felt to be in a kinetic relationship to one another. This was what the Greeks meant when they spoke of harmony.

But it is improbable that harmony, in the sense of two or more pitches sounded simultaneously, can exist without tonality. Even granting the use of consonances only, the ear requires a point of departure and a destination. As soon as one chord succeeds another this requirement becomes assertive. Only a recognition of tonality can satisfy it.

As is the case with every phenomenon of musical evolution, the evolution of harmony involved composer and listener alike. The present situation was reached by processes of disintegration in which composer and listener shared the flushed pleasures of over-indulgence in harmonic license and faced together the cheerless consequences of jaded sensibility.

The musical consonance is still felt as a pleasant sound. But the abuse of dissonance, and generations of light-hearted tampering with key-relationships, have robbed dissonance of its tonal properties of tension and suspense; and left it merely a tiresome ugliness. It has deprived modulation, the movement from one key to another, of the capacity to excite the exquisite anxiety associated with the momentary loss of tonal equilibrium that so fascinated the early admirers of Beethoven, Chopin, and Wagner.

Roger Sessions has given the following exemplary account of the compositional trends leading up to the present situation:

"Actually, the roots of the technical crisis in music may be traced far back into the past. They may be traced, if one likes, at least to the time when Bach, following the implications of tonality to logical conclusions, advocated the general adoption of the tempered scale. This led, as we all know, to the exploitation of an ever wider circle of key-relationships, and thus made possible the sonata form—what we call sometimes the 'symphonic' technique of Beethoven. The essence of this technique is the possibility it yields of organizing the sharpest contrasts.

"It made possible not only design of the largest possible span, by reason of the far-flung tonal relationships which it put at the composer's disposal, but it yielded also, quite inevitably, a far greater richness of detail on a smaller scale. For as bold juxtapositions of distantly related harmonies became familiar—and as the ear became accustomed to them— it became inevitable that composers should use them with less and less constraint. We may regard the development of music in the nineteenth century as, from one point of view, the result of the fact that composers found such highly charged juxtapositions exciting, and gained from them an apparently inexhaustible supply of new and even subtler nuances of expression . . .

"As of 1914—the year when the nineteenth century began to collapse—the musical world (the creative musical world, that is) was dominated by Debussy and Richard Strauss, whose music at that time seemed to carry the development of harmony as far as it could be carried within the limits of the tonal system. Strauss had recently written his 'Elektra,' and it was not yet evident that in his later works he would turn his back decisively on the harmonic daring and the expressive power which that work embodies. As for Debussy, he at that time considered his work as in some sense an act of rebellion against the confining principles of tonality, widely regarded by composers of that day as an encumbrance which had outlived its usefulness and of which composers had best rid themselves as quickly as possible . . .

"Music had developed to a point where its formerly valid premises, of which tonality was only one, had collapsed; in a sense they had collapsed of their own weight. The nineteenth century had run its course, and the composers were moved to discover new values to supersede it. . . . It was evident that the flood of new possibilities, or let us say new material, which music had acquired needed organization; that the nineteenth century development had led to a kind of anarchy for which the prevailing ideas of the time offered no principle of organization. The composers of the twenties felt very clearly that the freedom of resources they had acquired had been yielded ultimately by the classic tradition; that it had developed out of that tradition, which through its own inherent drive, had led beyond itself. It was not a question of repudiating this tradition but of organizing the sequel to it." [8]

This would seem to be a euphemistic way of indicating that the fight for harmonic emancipation turned out to have been a long, lusty crusade for the privilege of committing harmonic suicide. But it was not until they had practically destroyed the implications of tonality that composers suddenly discovered that emancipation had brought them, not freedom of musical speech, but the inability to speak musically at all. The tonal framework they had so hopefully destroyed proved to have been the very substance of their creative language. It was as if man had escaped the constraints of the earth's atmosphere only to discover that he could no longer breathe and must quickly find or devise another.

The composers themselves were the first to grasp the significance of what had happened, and their reactions were appropriately violent. Nor was it necessarily the younger men who sensed the trouble and led the reaction. Such old hands as Strauss and Debussy, alarmed at the emptiness ahead, the dreariness of the landscape toward which their own music was leading them, began looking nostalgically over their shoulders.

The leaders of the subsequent generation, notably Schön-berg, Stravinsky, and Bartok, who had started out flushed with confidence in an inherited wealth of technical resources and technical know-how, discovered that all that glitters technically is not necessarily music, and quickly dropped Wagner, Rimsky-Korsakoff, and Liszt in favor of Bach and Mozart.

The time had come when the twelve tones available to us could no longer offer new harmonic combinations or successions of combinations capable of stimulating new and stronger sensations. Every combination or succession of combinations was felt to be tolerable, if not pleasurable. The ear no longer capable of tonal outrage can no longer be fascinated by progression, excited by modulation, disturbed by dissonance, or assuaged by resolution and cadence. Where everything goes, nothing matters!

This is the case with the average ear today. It spells the end of tonal harmony, and this, in turn, spells the end of what we call serious music. The composer is no longer inhibited harmonically by any rules at all, unless he voluntarily subjects himself to the strictures of the twelve-tone system, but his emancipation does him no good. There is no longer any new harmony that can be musically effective. A century of abuse has exacted the full price. When serious music ceased to be harmonic, it ceased to be either musical or serious.

Honegger, speaking of contemporary music in general, has said: "What strikes me most forcibly is the haste of its reactions, its dependence on working methods. It took centuries to arrive at the free employment of the twelve tones. From this point on, further development suddenly adopted a fast tempo."[1] *

In view of the ample evidence that composers, better than anyone else, have understood the nature of the harmonic crisis, the haste of their reactions is not surprising. It is even less surprising when one learns just how precisely and how grimly they have appraised the fact and its consequences.

Honegger, for instance, reminded of a statement by the French critic, Emile Vuillermoz, that creative originality lies in the capacity to produce new harmony, remarks: "Think of the dead end to which such a formula drives us. If Vuillermoz is right, then that means that there can be no more great composers, since all the possible harmonic superimpositions have already been employed."[1] †

Similarly, Hindemith has written: "If anything seems to be of little reward, it is the search for originality in harmony. After a thousand years of research, experiment, and application, harmony has become thoroughly known; no undiscovered chord can be found. If we have to depend on novelty in harmony, we might as well write our last funeral march for the death of our own music.

"We may ask," he continues, "whether we could not assemble chords novel in their succession (even if not in their individual arrangement of tones) to produce less traditional patterns of sound. Would not such novelty in succession be proof of a further extensibility of the harmonic material,

* *Je suis compositeur,* by Arthur Honegger. Copyright by Editions du Conquistador, Paris, 1951.
† *Ibid.*

thus showing that the steadily ascending line of harmonic development had not reached its end? This idea, like so many others concerning musical styles and aesthetics, is extravagant, born of fancy, and defies reasonable investigation." [2]

The same might be said of most contemporary composition, which represents, after all, a similar kind of wishful thinking, if expressed in purely compositional terms. As Sessions has said: "If we should allow ourselves to regard music as essentially dead we would be confessing not only our inability to cope with its demands, but our unwillingness to do so. We would be, as it were, denying our creative impulse or confessing ourselves devoid of it. As long as composers feel impelled to express themselves, music will be alive, and it is for us, with all the vitality at our disposal, to make it flourish." [3]

The means by which composers seek to avoid a denial of their creative impulse are various, but they all have in common what Honegger has noted as a "dependence on working methods." The atonalists, or twelve-tonists, for instance, seek to continue the harmonic tradition by freeing harmony of tonal reference. In other words, their writing is multiple-voiced but without regard for the feeling for key and key-relationships which provided the structural basis of all previous Western music. Their syntax derives from a system of motives rather than a system of chords; but since they also insist on writing harmonically, or at least polyphonically, they experience difficulty in escaping harmonic or tonal connotations. Indeed, they usually fail, with results which Hindemith has described most picturesquely:

"To be sure, they do not, contrary to their conviction, eliminate tonality; they rather avail themselves of the same trick as those sickeningly wonderful merry-go-rounds on fair grounds and in amusement parks, in which the pleasure-seeking visitor is tossed around simultaneously in circles and up and down and sideways in such fashion that even the innocent onlooker feels his insides turned into a pretzel-shaped distortion. The idea is, of course, to disturb the customer's feeling of gravitational attraction by combining at any given moment so many different forms of attraction that his sense of location cannot adjust itself fast enough.

"So-called atonal music, music which pretends to work without acknowledging the relationships of harmonies to tonics, acts just the same as those devilish gadgets; harmonies both in vertical and in horizontal form are arranged so that the tonics to which they refer change too rapidly. Thus we cannot adjust ourselves, cannot satisfy our desire for gravitational orientation. Again spatial dizziness is the result, this time in the sublimated realm of spatial images in our mind. I personally do not see why we should use music to produce the effect of seasickness, which can be provided more convincingly by our amusement industry. Future ages will probably never understand why music ever went into competition with so powerful an adversary." [2]

Hindemith is wrong in one important respect. As a professional musician and composer, probably endowed with absolute pitch, he has a more acute sense of tonality than the average layman. The latter is less likely to suffer from the agitated sensations of the chute-the-chute than from the sensations of the untutored wanderer in a wasteland.

What bothers the layman is the absence of any landmarks, any of the familiar symbols of musical succor and sustenance. Hindemith has come closer to the layman's point of view when, in another connection, he writes: "A musical structure which, due to its extreme novelty, does not, in the listener's mind, summon up any recollections of former experiences, or which incessantly disappoints his constructive expectations, will prevent his creative cooperation." [91]

The twelve-tonists also weigh themselves down with a good deal of dogma, which presumably satisfies their craving for a more orderly musical world than the one into which they were born. This has not escaped the scorn of their non-conformist brethren. Honegger, for instance, observes: "They remind me of galley-slaves who, having thrown off their chains, voluntarily hang two hundred-pound balls on their feet in order to run faster." [1] Hindemith's comment is: "The idea of restricting oneself to an arbitrary system of tone combinations strikes me as being more doctrinaire than the rules of the most dried up diatonists. Is it not odd that the same composers who espouse harmonic freedom . . . have fallen, in structural matters, into a formalism compared with which the artifices of the early Netherlands contrapuntists are child's play." [35]

The neo-classicists, the neo-romanticists, and all the other neos, on the other hand, attempt to reconcile the modern approach to dissonance with the classical concept of tonality. This is possible only on paper, for tonality requires a tonal concept of dissonance, and the composer no longer treats dissonance tonally.

Thus we encounter a hilariously paradoxical situation in which the atonalist may often appear to be tonal, since by his very effort to avoid any combination which might produce a tonal effect, he calls attention to the tonal character of his failures. The neo-whatever-he-is, on the other hand, attempting to producing a consistent effect of tonality, but forced by fear of imitation to adhere to the modern concept of dissonance, renders the atonal effect of his failures doubly conspicuous.

The contemporary composer is, in short, caught between two fires, with all possible exits blocked. As a serious composer he is committed to the composition of music to which meaning can be attributed, or which is at least sufficiently extensive in form to warrant a claim to significance. It is also required of his music that it be original, that it support the assumption that music is still "an art in progress."

But harmony, without which neither the illusion of meaning nor the actuality of large forms in the traditional sense is possible, can no longer be used in a manner at once effective and original. The existing devices can not be used originally, and original devices are ineffective. It is a somber picture.

The composer persists in his search for the harmonic clue to the solution of his creative troubles. His chances of discovering anything worth the trouble are slim. It's more than looking for a needle in a haystack. All rational examination of the circumstances indicates that in this haystack there is no needle.

THE CRISIS OF MELODY

⋄ ⋄
⋄

ONE may ask why the contemporary composer, faced with Honegger's "wall of accumulated materials," does not go back to simple monodic melody. To ask the question is to misunderstand the implications of the harmonic crisis.

True, the crisis of polyphony in the sixteenth century was resolved by the rediscovery of an essentially monodic music, with chordal accompaniment added as a souvenir of the polyphonic tradition and as an accommodation to ears accustomed to multiplicity of voices.

But this is scant help to the serious composer today. He is the melodically anemic heir of generations of composers whose melodic invention was inhibited by the implicit primacy of harmonic considerations. His predecessors were guided, wittingly or unwittingly, by Vuillermoz's view that "creative originality lies in the capacity to produce new harmony." Their music derived its distinctive characteristics from harmonic novelty.

Thus the serious composer has little choice but to persist in seeking a harmonic rather than a melodic solution. He does so, not necessarily because he is incapable of inventing a good tune, but because his status as a serious composer is dependent upon his continuing, somehow, to write harmonically.

He recognizes instinctively that the European musical tradition, which it is his purpose to perpetuate, is distinctively harmonic, and that its continuity is impossible without an extension of harmonic resources. For a composer's appreciation of this problem we are again indebted to Hindemith:

"It was always harmony that fascinated musicians more than the other two elements, melody and rhythm. From about 900 through more than a thousand years we see an uninterrupted flow of harmonic discoveries and ever-changing applications of harmonic material. And even nowadays, when we might think that an all-round knowledge of musical material would teach us a well-balanced attention to every branch of technical and stylistic application, it is again harmony which is the musician's main concern. Hardly ever do we hear of attempts to invent new musical forms; the most radical inventors adhere to the traditional forms of the sonata and the symphony, and even such period pieces as minuets, sarabandes, etc., have had to be taken out of the moth-closet.

"Melody, although it is for the layman perhaps the most obvious and, in its effects, the most direct, of the three musical elements, has played a less important role in the experts' considerations. But harmony seems to everyone to be of such importance that many writers have almost nothing in their minds but the search for never-heard harmonies and harmonic progressions. You may read articles about modern music; periodicals may report about the fights between creative artists and their followers; music appreciation may instruct students about the progress of music in our time—the theme is mainly, and sometimes exclusively, harmony." [2]

It is not because it is no longer possible to write melodies within the existing scale system. The Hit Parade is all the evidence needed to prove the contrary. The melodic resources of our scales are by no means exhausted. It is rather that the kind of melody listeners like to hear is no longer integral to the late traditions of serious music, and has not been for about a hundred years.

It was possible for Mozart, Rossini, Weber, Donizetti, Bellini, and Verdi to write arias that were just as much song hits as *Star Dust, Summertime,* and *Some Enchanted Evening,* and which achieved on hand-organs and in every conceivable orchestra, band, and piano arrangement, a dissemination corresponding to that accomplished for hit tunes today by the radio, the phonograph, and the juke box. But first Beethoven and then Wagner taught the sophisticated music lover to regard such music as trivial, or at least incompatible with the concept of music's higher responsibilities in the field of philosophical and psychological articulation.

Although both Beethoven and Wagner produced their share of memorable tunes, it was their harmonies rather than their tunes that gave their music its special distinction. And it is not their most melodious music that is associated with their greatest achievements. Both Beethoven and Wagner were most melodious, or, to be more precise, most tuneful, in their earliest works. But the late sonatas and quartets are counted superior to the early sonatas, and the quartets from Opus 18. Similarly, *Parsifal, Tristan und Isolde* and *The Ring* are considered a great improvement on *Tannhäuser* and *The Flying Dutchman.* The reminders of Bellini in the latter have been the subject of a good deal of critical condescension.

To put it differently, Beethoven and Wagner, particularly in their later works, approached melody from a thematic rather than from a tuneful point of view. The distinction between a theme and a tune is essentially that the theme is thought of as something which lends itself to spatial development, as a source of significant inspiration. The tune is thought of as complete in itself, a miniature musical structure.

Thematic development has always been primarily a matter of harmony. Themes are chosen with a view to the richness of their harmonic properties and their suitability to the composer's structural project. This is one of the reasons why, in Beethoven's sketch books, so many themes are subjected to such painstaking alteration and revision. Beethoven was obviously concerned, not only with the qualities of the theme as a tune, but also with what it offered him in terms of harmonic-structural properties.

In music's classic period it was expected of a theme that it also be a good tune, but as harmonic considerations gained absolute primacy in the course of the nineteenth century, the tunefulness of a given theme became less and less important, while important themes became less and less tuneful.

Until Wagner's time the tune retained its respectable status, at least in the opera house. But Wagner's intensely propagated contempt for the conventions governing the lyric theater of his time, coinciding with the sanctity accorded the recently rediscovered more thoughtful than melodious last works of Beethoven, rendered suspect any popularity won by melodic accessibility.

All subsequent composition was influenced accordingly. Art music became less and less melodious. Even the melodious Verdi was conspicuously less tuneful after *Aïda*. He has been applauded for it by critics and connoisseurs ever since, although *Rigoletto*, *La Traviata*, *Il Trovatore*, and *Aïda* continue to be his most popular operas. Later Italian opera composers, among them Leoncavallo, Mascagni, Ponchielli, Cilea, Giordano, and Puccini, while never forsaking entirely the blandishments of a sustained vocal line, were less formally tuneful than their ancestors. Later generations of Italians have not been tuneful at all. In the symphonic world such tunesmiths as Tchaikovsky and Rachmaninoff, not to mention so recent a Russian as Prokofiev, have paid for the popularity of their tunes with a good deal of critical disparagement.

Much of what Wagner taught has since been rejected— and by no other segment of musical society with such vehemence and unanimity as by the fraternity of composers. But the reaction has been directed at his manner rather than at his method. Beginning with Debussy, composers to a man have scorned Wagner for the richness of his harmonies, the lusciousness of his orchestra, the length of his compositions and their intellectual pretentiousness—in short, for what is conveniently summed up as romantic transcendentalism, or as transcendental romanticism.

This reaction has been expressed in the Italian verismo opera, in the so-called impressionism of Debussy and Ravel, in the vigor and exotic color of the pre-World War I ballet scores, and in the neo-classical feeling that dominates all serious music written since 1920. In its simplest terms this reaction can be described, in the theater, as an effort to get back to human beings, to the naked drama of human life, and in the concert hall as an effort to get back to a more musical music, uninflated by descriptive and philosophical implications.

But the reaction could not disregard Wagner's harmonic advances. It might reject the manner and the purposes of their Wagnerian employment, but it could not escape the fact that the advances had been made, nor undo what they had done to the listening habits and the critical mores of the sophisticated musical public. Wagner himself was no mean melodist. The success of his great works would hardly have been possible without the tunes. How the tunes would have fared without the harmony is no longer a question of any importance, since to the lay listener the Wagnerian tune and the Wagnerian harmony are inseparable.

The paradox of Wagner's contribution to musical evolution is that, while he did more than any other single composer to destroy the tonal references from which harmony had evolved and by which it was governed in music's classic period, he also left both composer and listener more dependent on harmony than either of them had ever been before. In no other previous composer's work is the concept of melody so exclusively thematic, or the thematic development so intensely harmonic.

The key to Wagner's destructive work is his freedom of modulation. Prior to his time modulation was the principal factor of musical structure, the kinetic substance of the structural resources of tonal harmony. It was the movement from one key to another that provided the contrast and adventure essential to the sustenance of spacious design. A feeling for tonality on the part of the listener was a prerequisite for the full experience of the phenomenon of modulation.

With Wagner, however, modulation defies the strictures of tonality, and tends to become simply a succession of chords, melodically and tonally outrageous, but rich in a suggestion of harmonic color, and productive of what may be called a kaleidoscopic fascination. The harmonic verticals and the melodic lines and contours of previous musical structure, based on tonality, give way to an amorphous structure of color and mood.

Weighed down with the assumption of a higher calling than mere melody and rhythm could satisfy, but deprived of the structural support of strong tonal centers and the listener's instinctive acceptance of the validity of key relationships, music became more and more dependent upon harmonic novelty for the contrasts required to sustain large forms and to project the illusion of articulateness. This is why, throughout the latter part of the nineteenth century and the first quarter of the twentieth, harmonic idiosyncrasy is what distinguishes

any given composer's style and is the focal point of most critical analysis.

Composers in the eighteenth century were distinguished
from one another by their melodies and by the imagination
and skill with which they employed a harmonic idiom more
or less the common property of all. From roughly 1850 on-
wards harmony becomes the most prominent, sometimes the
exclusive distinguishing feature of a composer's style. Any
given composer's harmonic idiom was considered virtually
his private property, protected by right of discovery. Others
employing it were accused of imitation, if not of plagiarism.

This helps to explain why so many melodies from compositions of the second half of the nineteenth century and the
first quarter of the twentieth are unthinkable apart from their
harmonic setting. It explains why so much of this music
yields so little that can be retained in the memory and whistled or hummed, and why even that which is so retained is
whistled or hummed to a remembered harmony mentally
heard. With harmony thus dominant, and melody governed
by harmonic considerations, a falling off in the quality of
pure melodic invention was an obvious corollary, along with
a corresponding decline in the listener's melodic awareness.

It also explains why so many music-lovers today have more
respect than real enthusiasm for Bach, Handel, Mozart, and
Haydn, and why the music of these composers, particularly
that of Mozart and Haydn, is often dismissed by the layman
as "tinkly." The listener to serious music nowadays expects
to be assaulted by rich chords, instrumental and harmonic so-
norities and violent contrasts produced by startling progressions. This is the Wagnerian heritage. If expectation is seldom satisfied by modern music it is not because the listener
has lost his taste for it, or, indeed, his need for it. He is no
longer capable of the concentration required to follow and

appreciate a fine melody melodically developed, nor has he the awareness of tonality without which music of the classical period cannot be fully experienced and enjoyed.

This is a basic point of divergence between contemporary composers and their audiences. The contemporary composer neither can nor will continue in the direction taken by musical evolution from Beethoven to Strauss. The neo-classicists reject it without qualification, and even the twelve-tonists, while justifying atonality as the logical consequence of tonal disintegration, reject the esthetic assumptions that made it possible in the nineteenth century to hail the disintegration of tonality as progress.

Not so the listener. The very music which the contemporary composer most heartily despises is the bread-winner of every orchestra and opera house, every choral society and big-name recitalist in Europe and the Americas. If the contemporary composer cannot or will not offer any new harmonic thrills, then the listener must make do with the best the literature already in existence can offer, trusting to electrifying performance to add excitement to devices in themselves no longer electrifying. This is the essence of the contemporary musical scene.

Thus it is not surprising that those contemporary composers who have enjoyed some small measure of genuine popular success, men like Prokofiev, Shostakovich, Khatchaturian, Pfitzner, Egk, Sibelius, Respighi, Barber, Menotti, Kodaly, etc., are those whose attitude toward the inherited materials has been the least rebellious and whose music retains the largest proportion of the harmonic and instrumental substance that so endears the music of the preceding generations to a large public.

They are not the men taken most seriously as contemporary composers in the sense of being innovators and pathbreakers for the styles of the future. Nor have they solved any of the technical problems by which the contemporary composer is so beset. They have simply been ingenious enough to make do with salvage. They have produced what sufficed to buy themselves a period of grace and encourage the illusion that music is still "an art in progress." What they have written is neither very good nor very popular. But from an audience point of view it is the best of a bad lot and the only new music in which the listener can still keep his bearings.

Such music only postpones, it does not solve, the issue. The non-appearance of any younger composers capable of achieving even this modest success indicates that the period of grace may be drawing to a close. The issues remain the same: harmonic exhaustion, the synonymous relationship of serious music and harmonic music, and the disinclination of the serious composer to write the kind of music the listener can take seriously. The inescapable fact is that there is now no way of employing the inherited materials that does not sound trite and imitative, nor any way of rejecting them that does not represent a break with tradition.

The structural properties of tonal harmony have been so destroyed by a century and a half of abuse that it is no longer possible for the composer to achieve a large form intelligible as such to the listener. The last functional role of serious music is the sound-track, where the descriptive and psychologically articulate character of its late traditions may be turned to profitable use without the requirement of originality, and where its incapacity any longer to yield substantial forms is compensated by the form of the screen narrative.

The inevitably imitative flavor of sound-track music is no disadvantage, since the music makes no claim to independent validity or distinction; indeed, it is important that the music be associated with previous musical experience, for the spectator gives it little attention, and the processes by which he responds to it are almost wholly unconscious. Thus it is that most sound-track music reminds one of Wagner, Strauss, Debussy, Ravel, the early Stravinsky, and Prokofiev, while most modern music neither radically neo-classical nor atonal suggests the sound-track.

Popular music, including jazz, uninhibited by the requirement of harmonic originality and free to exploit what our traditional scales still have to offer in the way of original melodies, solved the harmonic problem melodically and rhythmically. Which is probably another way of saying that the song writer and the jazz musician—excluding, of course, the modern experimentalists—have simply left it alone. They found it possible to be original in other ways. The product of the American song writer from about 1910 to the present is proof enough that one can still be both articulate and original within our scales without having to dispense with traditional harmonic accessories. And the jazz musician has given these melodies an extra originality by an entirely new approach to articulate phrasing, assisted by the explicit beat and pulsative support of the rhythm section, by new instruments and by new ways of playing the old ones.

None of these opportunities was available to serious composers. They recognized them, to be sure, and in the twenties and thirties such eminent men among them as Stravinsky, Milhaud, Ravel and Copland tried to exploit them within the framework of serious compositions. They found that it could not be done. The break with the tradition to which they were committed was too great. Even had they been able to feel jazz properly, and even if it were possible to write jazz, the musicians for whom they wrote could not have played it. Even if they could have played it, the result would have been incompatible with the expectations of a serious music audience. The composers were condemned to a hybrid, effective neither as jazz nor as serious music.

The serious music audience, the community of so-called music-lovers, is harmonically conditioned. The music in which it finds pleasure is harmonically conceived. The characteristics of form and substance that are the basis of its claim to higher purpose and superior respectability derive from harmony.

The jazz audience, for the most part inexperienced in listening to serious music and unresponsive to its communication, is blessed with a more innocent approach to music. It is not surprising that for the innocent listener the eternal values of melody and rhythm should be decisive.

As long as the contemporary composer continues to give primacy to harmony, either tonal or atonal, contemporary music will not matter. And if he ceases to do so he can no longer enjoy whatever gratification and privileges he derives from his status as a serious composer. His music will have ceased to be serious in the conventional understanding of the term.

It is not with good tunes that he can make the only kind of reputation important to him as the lineal descendent of Beethoven.

THE CRISIS OF RHYTHM

THE only musical element which may be said to have rivaled harmony in the contemporary composer's technical preoccupations is rhythm.

This is not apparent in the composer's prose, in which harmony is discussed at length and rhythm only briefly, if at all. But it is apparent in his compositions, where rhythmic speculation and experimentation are almost as common as dissonance.

The reason is obvious. Of the basic musical elements—melody, harmony, and rhythm—the last has been the least highly developed and the least systematically exploited in European music. This is not to say that rhythm has not played an important role. It is rather that the rhythmic characteristics of European music have been determined by considerations in which rhythm either was not the primary factor or was not recognized as such.

While the European masters devoted intensive study to the development of harmony and orchestration, there is little evidence of a corresponding academic concern with rhythm. The rhythm of European music seems rather to have followed naturally and inevitably from harmonic and instrumental evolution.

This may seem strange, at first glance, to those who have struggled as musical amateurs with the problems of counting beats and measures and correctly calculating the time values of dotted notes. Nor would it seem to jibe with the size of the battery in the symphony orchestra, or with the fact that music's most important personage has been, for many years, a man whose primary function is to beat time.

One is tempted to say that both the necessity of counting time and the importance of the time-beater are symptoms of rhythmic debility. But the rhythmic peculiarities of European music should not be disparaged so glibly. The problem is not one of debility but rather of ambiguity. This rhythmic ambiguity derives from the fact that European music is an instrumental art born of a vocal art. The conflicting rhythmic requirements of vocal and instrumental music have plagued it from Monteverdi's time to the present day.

When art music and popular music met at the close of the exclusively vocal polyphonic period, the orchestra, in its primitive forms, entered music as a derivative of the dance band. Most of the instrumental music of the seventeenth and eighteenth centuries is an exploitation of popular dance forms, or is derived from dance forms. But the vocal traditions of the polyphonic period were not entirely discarded.

The conflicting claims of the free rhythm of purely vocal music and the exact rhythm of popular dance music have never been completely resolved. Indeed, it would hardly be correct to say that they have ever been generally recognized, much less understood. The question of rhythmic exactitude is a source of conflict between singer and instrumentalist to this day. It is usually resolved, if it is resolved at all, by a fine compromise that recognizes a strong feeling for the measure rather than slavish obedience to the beat as the highest form of musicianship in either instrumentalist or singer. This conflict is unknown in musical systems where the line between vocal and instrumental music is more clearly drawn.

European music enjoys the singular distinction of requiring

of the instrumentalist that he emulate the voice and of the singer that he emulate the instrument. It provides for the instrument a kind of music whose eloquence is such that a text is often implied, and for the singer a music in which the words often do not count. No other system than the European, however, is similarly burdened with such complications as harmony and counterpoint, which often require that the linear impulses of rhythm be compromised in favor of the vertical impulses of multiple-voiced composition.

In music of more essentially rhythmic character, such preoccupation with the beat as is betrayed by the invisible counting of the instrumentalist and the singer and the visible counting of the conductor would seem preposterous. In African and oriental systems the beat is there, and is felt as a sovereign pulsation by player and listener alike. Its preeminence among the basic musical elements is reflected by inventive systematization and variation that make European rhythms seem primitive by comparison and whose advanced state of development and cultivation is paralleled in European music only in harmony and instrumentation.

This sovereignty of the beat was true, more or less, of European music until fairly well on. With the rapid development of instrumental music in the seventeenth century the regular beat and the symmetrical rhythmic patterns of dance music gained an initial primacy. But it is doubtful that European music ever had the rhythmic inevitability of African and Asiatic musical systems, or even of jazz, whose larger ensembles achieve without a conductor a precision achieved in symphonic music only by the finest orchestras under conductors of the first class.

Throughout the seventeenth and eighteenth centuries the conductor was an inconspicuous figure, usually the concertmaster, or the composer at the harpsichord, with a coordinating and supervisory rather than an executive responsibility.

The rhythmic implications of this have been astutely summarized by Fritz Rothschild in a recent book, *The Lost Tradition in Music*: [36]

"It is important," he says, "to understand the difference between the seventeenth century conception of rhythm and that of the nineteenth century down to our own time. Today we usually think of rhythm as connected with the whole composition, as with a symphony, a sonata, a quartet, etc.; or if we analyze a smaller unit we sometimes speak of the rhythm of a melody or a phrase. Such a conception of rhythm, namely the rhythm of an entire piece or phrase, was unknown to the musician of the Old Tradition, and we look for it in vain in the literature on musical subjects of that period.

"There was, in fact, only one conception of rhythm—that of one single bar, and it was expressed by beats. The beats were given and not left ad libitum to the players, and they had nothing in common with dynamic accents (unknown at the time of the Old Tradition), nor were they rendered in a like manner; the distribution of the given beats had to be maintained through the entire piece. Neither composer nor interpreter could deliberately change the arrangements of these beats—rigidly governed by the conventions—unless he changed the time signature or the combination of note values or added other marks."

But this was before interpretation superseded execution as the objective of musical performance; in other words, before Beethoven. From Beethoven's time on, the purpose of music was conceived more and more in terms of meaning rather than movement. The rhythmic element, in the sense of a pattern of sustained pulsation in which performer and listener could participate equally, and with equal assurance that their rhythmic expectations would not be betrayed, receded into the background.

Rhythm of a kind, of course, there has always been. There can be no music without movement, and this movement must conform to a pattern of some sort if the listener is to participate. But with the change of emphasis in performance from self-evident execution to speculative interpretation, both composer and listener began to look for more sophisticated sources of dynamic movement than the insistent pattern of a drum beat.

Historically this represented a swing back to the vocal concept of rhythm, to the plastic melodic phrase molded expressively by a singer employing free rhythmic devices derived from poetry and speech to make the phrase articulate. But it occurred in an art whose instrumental character was already established, and which was already burdened with a numerous ensemble. The execution of music conceived rhapsodically, and tending to a vocal concept of rhythm, could not be left to the discretion of fifty or sixty individuals, each with his own interpretive ideas and convictions.

Music was moving into a phase where, as Ralph Kirkpatrick has put it so well, "the essential expressive quality of a melodic interval lies not in the notes themselves, but in the space between the notes, in the manner in which one gets from one note to another." [37]

What lies between the notes is something about which no two musicians are likely to agree. The singer, or the instrumental soloist, can act at his own discretion, but when large ensembles are required to accept this conception of melodic movement, there has to be an arbiter.

At this point the conductor became necessary. He was required to reconcile, not only the differences of opinion between individual musicians playing the same music, but also the infinite interpretive conflicts and ambiguities present in any given piece of music, a consequence of the evolution of a vocal concept of composition from an instrumental art.

While conceived vocally in terms of its epic, rhapsodic, or contemplative character, this music was conceived instrumentally in terms of execution. Its composers were instrumentalists who thought in terms of instruments, and whose greatest instrument was the symphony orchestra.

The initial clash of vocal and instrumental concepts in the seventeenth century had been resolved in favor of the instruments, and particularly in favor of the orchestra. The instruments, which had begun as voice substitutes, replaced the voice as the dominant executive factor in music. The solo singer satisfied the taste for monodic melody that had ended the dominance of polyphony, while instrumental music satisfied the Western ear's requirement for multiple-voiced composition, a carry-over from the polyphonic era.

The rhythmic conflict resulting from the collision of an instrumental, or dance type of strict time with the older vocal type of free time was reconciled through the device of recitative, a concession to the singer's requirement that the expressive faculties of song be uninhibited by the rhythmic insistence of a relentless beat and to the audience's requirement for relief from uniform rhythms. The recitative made it possible, within the framework of a composition dominated by the instrumental concept of rhythm, to set off areas in which rhythmic refinements were left to a soloist's discretion.

The solution was, in short, a compromise. It demanded adjustments from singer and orchestra alike, but it left both with fixed and mutually respected opportunities for the unrestricted exercise of their respective rhythmic predilections. The singer's opportunity was the recitative, the orchestra's the overture and the various instrumental interludes or sinfonias from which eventually evolved the three- and four-movement symphony.

The compromise was satisfactory as long as instrumental music retained its purely instrumental character. It even survived the emergence of the orchestra as the dominant and representative executant of European music. The device of recitative was retained, and solo instruments even adopted it. Singers had long since learned to adjust to the instrumental style in music where the equal participation of instruments made rhythmic precision essential.

What brought on the new crisis in the nineteenth century was not a conflict between singer and orchestra. It was rather the tendency of composers, from Beethoven's time on, to require of the orchestra that it achieve a vocal type of expression. Without consciously generalizing the recitative formula, composers gave to orchestral music an increasingly expressive character.

In a word, a musical art now dominated by instruments began to find its destiny in a vocal concept of musical expression. The vocal and instrumental concepts of rhythm were again in conflict, but the problem was to reconcile, not the differences between singer and orchestra, but the differences between one player in the orchestra and another. A new intermediary agent was needed, and it was found in the person of the conductor.

Through him it was possible to achieve a rhythmic flexibility, combined with precision, that would have been impossible had the individual members of the orchestra been left to their own devices. Under a good conductor it was now vouchsafed to the orchestra to achieve a plastic line previously accessible only to the singer or, occasionally, to an instrumental soloist imitating vocal style. In the most basic terminology it may be said of the conductor that his role in history has been to make a singer out of a dance band.

Of all elements of music, rhythm is the most difficult to discuss, if only because it is so difficult to define. To draw the line between melody and rhythm, for instance, is impossible, since melody, in more than the purely detached sense of a series of higher and lower pitches, cannot exist without some sort of rhythm. Even harmony, through its dynamic properties, can have a rhythmic function. The movement from tonic to dominant and dominant to tonic is almost certain, unless artificially frustrated, to develop a rhythmic pattern.

For the purpose of this discussion, however, which is to seek some insight into the contemporary composer's problems, it should suffice to accept rhythm as referring to that element of music which has to do with movement, the functions of movement, and the governing of movement. Since the composer's problems arise from his inherited materials, with respect to rhythm no less than with respect to harmony, they can be understood only in terms of what has previously occurred.

This can best be understood by comparing familiar compositions in their proper chronology with an eye to their movement characteristics. Almost any series of compositions selected at random will do. Compare, for instance, a Brandenburg Concerto with a tone poem by Strauss. Compare *The Marriage of Figaro* with *Falstaff*. Compare a symphony by Haydn or Mozart with a symphony by Brahms, Bruckner, or Mahler. Compare *Fidelio* with *Wozzeck*.

Several rhythmic facts are immediately obvious. The earlier pieces move more easily and more spontaneously. They are less dependent upon an urge to move communicated and regulated by a determined conductor. The pulsation seems to originate, not in the conductor's beat, but in the music itself. One has the feeling with the older music that an orchestra, given the beat, could carry on without further prodding, guidance, or control. With Bruckner and Mahler one feels that the orchestra, without the conductor, would not make much progress.

There are other than rhythmic reasons for this. As the nineteenth century drew to a close, the richness of the harmonic idiom and the obesity of the modern orchestra tended to inhibit horizontal movement. Music moved less easily simply because there was more of it to move. And movement became less essential as the dynamic substance in the vertical phenomenon of the chord superseded the horizontal dynamics of the rhythmic pattern.

But there were rhythmic reasons, too. One feels in the later music that the objective is more plastic, that what counts is not the structure that grows naturally out of a self-evident blend of rhythmic, melodic, and harmonic factors, but rather a design molded by the conductor from an accumulation of rhythmic, melodic, and harmonic elements left at the conductor's disposal for the accomplishment of the composer's expressive purpose. This is the vocal concept of rhythm. It shows us the conductor, not only as the man who makes the orchestra sing, but also as music's supreme singer.

Another way of understanding this is simply to look at the scores. The older ones are innocent of expression marks, the later ones full of them. The inference is that in the older works the sheerly structural problem was solved in the printed score. Assuming a reasonably just tempo, the harmonic and melodic structural elements cannot help but assert themselves. They are present in such a way that a person of adequate technical competence and normal musicality cannot escape their implications.

The significance of this in a consideration of rhythm is the fact that, once an older piece is set in motion, architecture takes place automatically. The structural elements are all present, properly assorted and measured. With no more than the establishment of a beat they begin to fall easily and inevitably into place. To put it even more simply, the form is ready made. It needs only the rhythmic pulse to give it life.

This has been true of very little serious music since Beethoven's time, and it is certainly not true of most of that music which has been regarded as the greatest. This is accountable only in part to the general musical trend toward a harmonically vertical rather than melodically linear kind of dynamism. This trend has existed, to be sure, but it was not the only source of new dynamic effects, nor even the most important. Along with the dynamism yielded by unexpected chords and modulations came another dynamism yielded rhythmically, not by momentum, but by its interruption.

This is the essence of recitative. In its simplest form recitative merely permits the singer to be rhythmically free. He uses this freedom, not just to escape the tedium of counting time, nor to abandon rhythm altogether, but rather to alter the rhythmic pulse for expressive effect. It is a device of dynamics, and it gains its dynamic effects by keeping the listener in doubt as to what the pulsation is to be, by anticipating or disappointing his rhythmic expectations.

Thus it was that in the nineteenth century all music became more or less recitative, sometimes, as in the major symphonies and operas of the century, on a colossal scale. The development culminated logically in the great recitative operas of Wagner and Verdi, in the tone poems of Liszt and Strauss, and in the epic symphonies of Brahms, Tchaikovsky, Bruckner, and Mahler.

It was at this time, as we have seen, that the conductor became essential. Recitative is a solo proposition, and it can be accomplished by large organizations only if all concerned conform to the discretion of a single voice. When the rhythmic patterns of orchestral composition were regular and predictable, even a fairly large band could maintain cohesion, since everyone shared the same pulsation and the same rhythmic expectations. But as music became recitative, or dramatic, it looked to the unexpected for dramatic effect.

Anyone who has been subjected to the unexpected braking of an automobile or elevator, or been suddenly precipitated into motion at an unwonted speed, has learned how exciting an unanticipated rhythmic deviation can be. This is the rhythmic significance of the *sforzandi, accelerandi, allargandi, morendi, ritardandi, rubati, fermate, a tempi,* etc., in which the scores of the nineteenth century abound. They all refer to the interruption or alteration of an established rhythm.

In short, what the nineteenth century did to harmony it also did to rhythm. What it did to the listener's tonal sensibilities it also did to his rhythmic sensibilities. And the end result was similar. An approach to rhythm based on the contradiction rather than the accommodation of the listener's rhythmic expectations led to a situation where his rhythmic feeling was unresponsive to further abuse. The listener who found any harmony tolerable, if not necessarily pleasurable, reacted with the same indifference to any new rhythmic adventure.

Thus the contemporary composer was faced with a rhythmic problem identical with the problem he faced in harmony: an exhausted resource to which he was committed by a tradition he could not deny.

But the simple solution would have been to return to a simple, steady beat, easily recognized and participated in by the listener. This is still possible, just as simple melodization and simple harmonization are still possible. It is not that the listener has lost his capacity to find pleasure in a simple melody, a simple harmony, or a simple rhythm. It is rather that he has lost the capacity to be much affected by deviations from simplicity.

This solution of the rhythmic problem is as impossible for the contemporary composer as is the melodic solution to his harmonic problem. He would find himself writing popular music instead of the emotionally, dramatically, intellectually, and graphically expressive music expected of him as a serious composer. His problem is complicated by the fact that, while this latter kind of music may be the kind expected of him, it is not the kind he particularly wants to write.

Another possibility would be to adopt a completely recitative style, to accept whole-heartedly the vocal concept of rhythm. This is even more repellent, for it puts the emphasis on expression rather than on design, and the contemporary composer is nothing if not a formalist. It is against precisely the expressive character of the music of the nineteenth century that he rebels.

His distaste for the vocal concept is intensified by the importance it attaches to the performer as an interpreter. The composer resents the intrusion of the performer as an interpretive agent betweeen himself and the listener. The strict rhythms of the instrumental concept offer the advantage of reducing the expressive element in music and making of the performer an executive rather than an interpreter.

Our century has seen the trend toward the vocal concept of rhythm, which persisted throughout the nineteenth century, reversed in favor of the beat. This has been reflected in serious music by the high percentage of ballets among the relatively successful scores of the century, and in popular music by the emergence of the dance band as the representative orchestra. Even in its songs, American popular music seldom loses sight of the popular taste for a rhythmic scheme in which the listener can participate.

The composer's problem derives from the fact that he cannot fulfill his assumed responsibilities as a writer of serious music simply by composing ballets. The proper setting for his music is the concert hall or the opera house, and his proper audience is one which comes, not to look, but to listen. The serious music audience, moreover, regards the prominent, obvious beat of popular music as primitive.

Faced with his own predilection for the instrumental concept of rhythm and his audience's prejudice against the obvious, the composer has come up with a compromise. It pleases nobody, but it at least preserves the reputation for complexity essential to the superstition that the serious composer is somehow superior to the simple fellows who write music that gives pleasure.

The compromise is to emphasize rhythm, but in a sophisticated way. The composer rejects the four-beats-to-the-measure, four-measures-to-the-period type of rhythmical symmetry which is the dance music basis of European instrumental music. To accept it, as long as he chooses to emphasize rhythm, would bring him close to conformity in the popular sense and to triviality in the serious sense. He chooses, instead, to regard this symmetry as the "tyranny of the bar line" and to defy it accordingly.

This breaking of the bar line has been matched in futility only by the composer's efforts to break the bonds of tonality by evolving an atonal system. In both cases the composer has got himself into a fix where he is more dependent than ever upon just those technical elements from which he sought emancipation. No composers have been so hamstrung by problems of harmony as the atonalists, and no composers have been so tortured by the problems of rhythm as those who broke the bar line.

It is not, so far as rhythm is concerned, that the bar line might not well be broken. It is an artificial device. The important thing in rhythm is not the symmetrical pattern, of which the bar line is a symbol, but the establishment of a pulse. The symmetrical pattern is of melodic rather than rhythmic origin. And the bar line is a convenience in keeping track of melodic rather than rhythmic progress.

Indeed, the composer's revolt was not so much against the bar line itself as against the regularity of its occurrence. Thus, in place of the traditional adherence to consecutive measures, each measure with the same number of beats, he experimented with a kind of rhythm in which the number of beats to the measure was constantly changed.

His purpose was to emphasize the rhythmic character and content of his music by providing greater rhythmic variety. To put it in terms of the historical perspective, he attempted to replace the variety inherent in the vocal concept of rhythm, but dependent upon the performer for realization at the performer's discretion, with a variety determined and worked out by the composer, leaving nothing to the performer but the job of counting beats and measures.

His accomplishment was to deprive his music of rhythmic intelligibility. The harmonic catastrophe was duplicated by a rhythmic catastrophe. By denying the listener a tonal frame of reference, the effort to free music of tonality left the listener incapable of harmonic participation. Similarly, the effort to free rhythm of the constraints of easily recognized patterns deprived the listener of a rhythmic frame of reference and rendered his rhythmic participation impossible.

Here again we have confirmation from the thoughtful Honegger.

"I myself," he wrote, "remain very skeptical about these rhythmic refinements. They have no significance except on paper. They are not felt by the listener. . . . After a performance of Stravinsky's *Symphony in Three Movements* the players in the orchestra all remarked: 'One has no time to listen or appraise. One is too busy counting eighth notes.' Dependence upon the metronome robs the composer and the interpreter of any freedom. . . . What counts today is rhythmic shock, not melodic beauty." [1] *

Honegger forgot to add that even shock is no longer effective. The audience is as numbed rhythmically as it is numbed harmonically. Shock is no solution, at least not to

* *Je suis compositeur,* by Arthur Honegger. Copyright by Editions du Conquistador, Paris, 1951.

the composer. The performer, particularly the conductor, still draws dividends from shockingly fast tempi, but this has nothing to do with composition.

But the truth of what Honegger says about the interpreter must be readily acknowledged by any layman who has watched a virtuoso conductor do a Brahms symphony and then watched the same conductor do a modern work. The Brahms will have been largely a choreographic performance, the movement of the hands, arms, and body communicating not only the beat but also the conductor's interpretation of the music being played. It is the conductor's way of being a singer. In the modern composition he will have been preoccupied almost exclusively with the problem of marking time and giving entrances. In short, if the romantics made of the conductor a supreme singer, the moderns seem bent on turning him into a metronome.

For the listener to participate in this music would require that he become a metronome, too. To expect him to do so is as unrealistic as to hope that he will ever recognize the mirror and crab figures the atonalists so delight in fashioning from their twelve-tone rows, or that—assuming the possibility of recognition—he would find them particularly edifying.

THE CRISIS OF THE ORCHESTRA

THE executive glory of Western music is the symphony orchestra. Next to harmony it is also Western music's most prominently distinctive feature.

The orchestra is the instrument for which the symphonies of Haydn, Mozart, Beethoven, Schubert, Mendelssohn, Schumann, Brahms, Tchaikovsky, Bruckner, and Mahler were written. Without it the tone poems of Berlioz, Liszt and Strauss, the tone-paintings of Debussy and Ravel, the music-dramas of Wagner and the later operas of Verdi would be unthinkable.

When one thinks or speaks of music as a cultural ornament of Western civilization, it is almost inevitably in terms of the symphony orchestra. This is especially true of the United States, whose only serious claim to classical musical distinction lies in the wonderful orchestras of Philadelphia, New York, Boston, Chicago, San Francisco, and a dozen other cities. In Europe the orchestra is rivaled as an institution by the opera, but the distinction is unessential. Opera and orchestra are inseparable.

Were it not for the example already offered by harmony, one would be tempted to note it as odd .that the very instrument which provided the art of music with so many of the materials essential to its greatest achievements should also have provided so many of the elements of decay and dissolution which disfigure the art music of our own time. But to do so would be to overlook the symphony orchestra's origin in harmony.

What distinguishes the symphony orchestra from the instrumental ensembles of other musical systems is its original function as a multiple-voiced substitute for polyphonic or harmonically conceived song. Its growth and ultimate form were shaped by requirements originating in the harmonic nature of European music. Every musical system has some sort of orchestra. It provides rhythmic impulse and variety of tonal color, and its instruments are called upon occasionally to function as a voice substitute. But just as the absence of part singing and the exclusive dominance of the solo human voice, or choral song in unison, have barred other systems from any evolutionary course comparable to that of European music, so also have they rendered out of the question a growth of their instrumental ensembles along lines comparable to the symphony orchestra.

The harmonically functional role of the orchestra in Western music is reflected in such familiar orchestra-substitutes as the piano, the organ, the accordion, the harmonica, etc., and in such older instruments as the harpsichord and clavichord. While one may, nowadays, think of harmony and instrumentation separately, and study them as only distantly related techniques, they are, in fact, historically, functionally, and fundamentally inseparable. Every step in the evolution of harmony from the seventeenth century to the twentieth has been executed either by the orchestra or by an orchestra-substitute—that is, by a keyboard instrument. From Beethoven's time onward, harmonic evolution has been, to a great extent, not only orchestrally executed, but also orchestrally conceived.

Combined with harmony, the symphony orchestra provided fabulous resources of color, dynamics, rhythmic emphases, harmonic fulfillment and, above all, sonority. The fascination exercised upon the growing bourgeois audience of the nineteenth century by exciting harmonic experimentation in chords, chord progressions, and modulation was intensified through the resources of the orchestra. The suggestive faculties of novel harmonic combinations as played on the piano were nothing compared with the suggestive faculties of the same combinations played by an orchestra. Their occasional harshness was softened by discreet distribution among instruments of appropriately diverse range and character, their richness intensified by saturation in rich orchestral sound.

As exploited by the great orchestra composers of the last half of the nineteenth century, these resources brought both composer and audience to a point where orchestration began to be confused with composition, where the distinction between musical art and musical artifice was lost in the intoxication of an unexampled variety and wealth of orchestral color and the deafening splendor of orchestral noise.

By the end of the first quarter of the twentieth century not much was left but artifice. By the end of the second quarter artifice, too, was well along in decay. Not even harmony had proved so rich a source of devices as the orchestra for disguising and camouflaging the symptoms of musical creative decrepitude. The seductive effect of this kaleidoscopic apparatus upon composers and public alike has been well described by Hindemith:

"It is undeniably impressive to see scores of people work for one's entertainment or enlightenment, and a piece of music, be it of the worst kind, can hardly be thought of as being devoid of any value, since it was designed to be accepted for a representation in so glorious a frame. The mastermind who, with his harmonized fancies, keeps this mechanism humming doubtless knows his reasons for all these strange goings-on. Besides, we do not want to hurt our self-respect by admitting that with our dignified presence we are assisting something base and worthless. How could it be worthless if so many artists and instruments are employed? See what they have marshaled! Rows of fiddles, an impressive phalanx of basses, shiny brass tubing galore, an entire family of kettle drums, several pianos and other menacing keyboard instruments, not to mention the six busy men in the percussion section.

"Poor Bach and poor Haydn! You did not know how to capture an audience, and your scanty-looking orchestra pieces are just good enough as mere preparations for more demonstrative exhibits. Poor oratorio singers! You may appear in hordes, dressed in alluring gowns and singing like cherubs, but you cannot compete with the illustrious diligence of the full orchestra. And poor adagio movements, in which everyone plays unattractive long notes without much motion of fingers, bows, valves, sticks and keys, and with many players waiting idly for cues anyway. Ah, torrential cascades from the gargoyles of the orchestra! Ah, ocean full of roaming prodigies! Ah, Manhattanesque assembly of pipes, strings, reeds, and membranes!

"The provider of all these inadequacies, the trivial tone compiler, enjoys all the advantages of a situation circumscribed by works of genius and meant to be saturated with masterworks. Thus being in his own status already out of proportion with his surroundings, it is not too surprising to see disproportion cropping up in all his musical creations." [2]

The effect on musical form of preoccupation with harmonic effect has been noted, and particularly the tendency to substitute an amorphous structure of color and mood for the classical elements of harmonic verticals and melodic-rhythmic lines and contours. Without the orchestra this development would have been impossible, at least in the same degree. For the combination of harmonic and orchestral resources gave to an amorphous structure a dynamic formal substance of sheer sound.

It is customary to speak of modern orchestration as having begun with Berlioz. This is true as far as pure orchestration is concerned. It was the *Symphonie Fantastique* that pointed the way to a type of composition built around harmonic and orchestral metamorphoses of a single theme in defiance of traditional concepts of form. But the musical trend of which the orchestra proved to be the decisive instrument may more properly be said to have begun with Beethoven.

With him began the intensive exploitation of those dramatic faculties inherent in the diatonic scale that have contributed more than anything else to the popular assumption that music "means" something. With him began the development of dynamics as a decisive element in musical structure. The great provider of dynamic effects was the symphony orchestra.

Beethoven was not, certainly, the first composer to write dramatic music. There is drama in the operas of Gluck, Mozart, and even Cherubini. But Beethoven was distinguished from the others in that almost all his music was dramatic. Whereas earlier composers could, when the situation required, write dramatically, Beethoven could hardly write otherwise. His was a dramatic style, and he could not help but write dramatically. Pertinent in this connection is Paul Henry Lang's comment:

"We still do not realize the tremendous impact of Beethoven's music on the succeeding generations. We know that instrumental music was under his spell for the rest of the century, but there is still no department of music that does not owe him its very soul. Beethoven endowed pure instrumental music with the most intense and expressive dramatic accents, an expressiveness that cast its reflection on dramatic music itself. A circle closes here; opera-born symphony now helps to create the language of the modern music drama. The tremendous power and sharp edge of this music, its fervor and warmth, but, above all, its animated contrasts were eminently dramatic." [4]

Lang's observation that "opera-born symphony now helps to create the language of modern music drama" is especially perspicacious. He could have afforded to be even more pat. He could have said: "Opera-born symphony becomes symphony-born opera." From Beethoven's time onward all symphonic music was to become, in view of its prevailing dramatic and descriptive substance, operatic, while opera, at the same time, was to become increasingly symphonic.

Throughout the first half of the nineteenth century the concept of opera as a form in which singers are the protagonists was to hold its own, despite the steady growth of the orchestra in size and importance in the works of Weber, Meyerbeer, and Verdi. But after Wagner the scales were tipped irrevocably in favor of the symphonic concept. The orchestra became the protagonist, and responsibility for dramatic continuity and articulation shifted from the stage to the pit.

In its modest origins in the seventeenth century Italian opera the orchestra provided an opportunity for part-playing by instruments of different timbres and ranges. It gave singers a more plastic, more flexible, more mobile, more expressive, more varied, and less obtrusive accompaniment than was possible on instruments plucked or struck. It also provided an opportunity for varying a predominantly vocal entertainment with instrumental interludes, an opportunity that was, in the course of time, to lead to orchestral independence—hence Lang's reference to the "opera-born symphony." To the basic string quartet the wood winds added variety of color and the contrasts that made multiple-voiced part-writing easier to follow. The brass added brilliance and emphasis, and the percussion instruments provided the essential rhythmic impulse and punctuation.

Mozart and Haydn drew upon all these resources and achieved an instrumentation, not only beautifully balanced in sound, but also beautifully balanced in purpose. Theirs was a symphony orchestra perfectly designed to serve the expression of musical thought and musical invention, and perfectly employed by the composers in that service. Just as they perfected the resources of tonal harmony, worked out and passed along to them by hundreds of seventeenth and eighteenth century Italian, German, French, and English composers culminating in Bach, so also they perfected the essentially musical resources of the orchestra, developed by the same imaginative and adventurous creative spirits.

They also perfected the instrumental forms that had slowly developed from the suites, sonatas, toccatas, sinfonias, concerti grossi, and overtures of their predecessors, and evolved the classical symphony. It was to serve structurally as a model for emulation or as a point of departure for every composer who came after them.

Speaking of the period prior to Haydn and Mozart, William Wallace, in his excellent article on orchestration in Grove's Dictionary, remarks:

"Composers appear to have been occupied more with the construction of their theme than with the manner of presenting it. Lully was content to write the melody and the bass, leaving the middle parts, and such scoring as was requisite, to his copyists. . . . Gretry was equally indifferent, and it was said of his scores that you could drive a coach and four between the treble and the bass."

After Haydn and Mozart there could be no more talk of leaving the scoring and the filling in of middle voices to copyists and apprentices. For in these details, rather than in thematic invention and structure, lay the substance of future musical creation and individual stylistic distinction. After Beethoven, who may be said to have straddled the gap between the eighteenth and nineteenth centuries, came Berlioz and the whole history of evolutionary development that could make it possible, less than a hundred years later, for a Rimsky-Korsakov to say that "to orchestrate is to create" and prompt a Schönberg to attempt, in the third of his Five Orchestra Pieces, Opus 16, an experiment in which tone color is the sole substance. Again to cite Wallace:

"While the orchestra was growing in strength, its development was to have a profound effect upon composition. The art was being rent within itself by discord. Five years after the first performance of Beethoven's *Choral Symphony* there came the *Symphonie Fantastique* of Berlioz. The one was incomprehensible to many, the other devastating. Whatever the views that were held, it is clear that a rift had appeared, and that tradition on its complacent side had received a shock. . . . Some felt that the frontier of music had been extended."

The significance of this is subsequently more precisely defined when, in dealing with Berlioz, Wallace states: "It is not certain where composition with him ended and orchestration began."

In short, the "infallible test of the piano" was no longer applicable. Mozart's and Haydn's orchestral compositions all sound well when played on the piano, and give musical pleasure. For they are derived from purely musical elements of melody and rhythm, and the structure is fundamentally harmonic. The same may be said in lesser degree of Beethoven, Schubert, Schumann, and Brahms. At least, their orchestral music has had extensive and profitable currency in two- and four-hand piano arrangements. It cannot be said of Berlioz, Liszt, Wagner, Strauss, Bruckner, and Mahler.

Herein lies the explanation of the curious circumstance

that those critics in the nineteenth century who espoused Mendelssohn, Schumann, and Brahms were considered reactionary even though the composers themselves were contemporary and far from mere imitators of their hallowed predecessors. Both Schumann and Brahms made their respective contributions to the extension of harmonic freedom. Their music may correctly be regarded, in the conventional sense, as representing an advance over the music of, say, Beethoven and Schubert. They were even dramatic in the sense of the word as it applies to the instrumental music of Beethoven.

The question was rather one of definition. As Wallace says, "A rift had appeared." Brahms and Schumann, for all the romantic-dramatic elements in their music, remained true to the classical concepts of musical form based on melodic, harmonic, and rhythmic structure. The others tended toward a concept of form deriving from elements rather philosophical, psychological, literary, poetic, or graphic than musical—in other words program music, or the tone poem.

The great line of composers of musical music may be said to have ended with Brahms. After him the line between symphony and symphonic poem becomes blurred, no matter how careful such subsequent composers of symphonies as Tchaikovsky, Dvorak, Franck, Bruckner, Mahler, and Sibelius may have been to designate their symphonies as such and to underline the designation by adherence to the conventional three- or four-movement structural plan.

Not that there was no music in tone poetry. It continued to exploit musical elements of melody, harmony, and rhythm, but the expression could no longer be regarded as purely musical. Or, to put it more precisely, what was thus musically expressed was intended and assumed to be something more than merely music. Tone poetry was inspired by a literary model, by a poem, a picture, a vision, a philosophical concept, or a psychological problem, and was supposed to project a musical approximation or representation, a paraphrase, as it were, of the literary or graphic original.

The basic, indispensable instrument of tone poetry was the orchestra. This was not, to be sure, the orchestra of Haydn and Mozart, but the orchestra of Berlioz, Liszt, and Wagner. Schumann and Brahms would live on through their vocal, solo instrumental, and chamber music if all the symphony orchestras in the world were abolished tomorrow. But what would be left of the others, of Berlioz, Liszt, Wagner, Strauss, Bruckner, Mahler, and even Schönberg and Berg?

Nothing of any consequence! To say that they orchestrated rather than composed is a tempting but inadmissible generalization, although it is certainly true of many of their inferiors. But it is not too much to say that their works were conceived orchestrally. Removed from the orchestra, they are incapable of effectiveness on their purely musical substance alone.

Whereas Mozart, Haydn, Beethoven, Schubert, Mendelssohn, Schumann, and Brahms used the orchestra as a means of enrichment, the others used it rather as a means of articulation. Where the classicists thought in terms of musical effects orchestrally executed, the others began to think of instrumental effects more or less musically ordered. Whatever was done was considered justified as long as the "effect" was enhanced or heightened. Sound rather than purely musical organization became the sustaining substance of composition, and orchestration became a basic structural element. This accounts for the present conventional disparagement of transcription and its sanctimonious extension to the obviously transcription-proof music of older composers who made a habit of transcribing for any handy combination anything they thought worth the effort.

For the student of contemporary music the significant factor is that in the long, drawn-out battle between the classicists and the romanticists, or between the musicians and the tone poets, the latter carried the day and determined the course of musical evolution up to the time of the First World War.

As a consequence, the contemporary composer inherited an overgrown and unwieldy instrument whose size was incommensurate with economic circumstances and vastly out of proportion to what is required for musical articulation. As employed by Bruckner, Mahler, and the early Schönberg, its complement and employment was such as to call forth such adjectives as colossal, gigantic, mammoth, and cyclopean, while its functions were described in such non-musical terminology as palette, chiaroscuro, scene-painting, luminous, diaphanous, opalescence, fluorescence, etc. Rimsky-Korsakov even set up a tabulation of orchestral color combinations.

A reaction was inevitable. Not even this highly organized, numerous, and expert collective instrument could transcend the transcendentalism of Mahler's *Symphony of a Thousand.* It was capable of no more exact and specific graphic and prosaic description than Strauss' *Sinfonia domestica.* It could yield no more lustrous canvases than Debussy's *La mer* and *Iberia.* It could provide no more romantic philosophic pretentiousness than Schönberg's *Gurrelieder.* Stravinsky's *Le sacre du printemps* marked the limit of brutal primitive stylization. In *Daphnis and Chloë* Ravel offered the ultimate in orgiastic pagan riotousness. *Salomé* and *Elektra* had touched the extremes of sexual pathology, and *Der Rosenkavalier* seemed to define the limits of artistically tolerable lushness.

Obviously, this arrival at the outward limits of music's capacities in the dramatic and descriptive directions pointed by Beethoven and Berlioz was not a purely orchestral phenomenon. It was part and parcel of a general exhaustion involving the whole problem of harmonic substance and structure. But the orchestra had provided the last rich technical resource, and had made possible a last few glorious years of grace following Wagner's raid on the capital resources of chromatic harmony.

The reaction that set in after the First World War had two odd characteristics. The first was that it was precipitated, not by a change in popular taste, but by a change in the creative orientation of composers. The second was that the composers who led it—Schönberg, Strauss, Bartok, Stravinsky, and Ravel—were all men who had participated in the apotheosis of the orchestra's "Götterdämmerung." The public had not complained, and to this day orchestral music of that ultimate period is among the most viable in the standard repertoire. It was the composers who rebelled.

A Schönberg, whose *Gurrelieder* had required twenty-five wood winds and twenty-five brass, turned to a chamber orchestra of as few as fifteen instruments. Stravinsky, whose *"Le sacre"* had employed eighteen each of wood winds and brass, reacted similarly. Even Strauss, whose *Sinfonia domestica,* had called for a piccolo, three flutes, two oboes, oboe d'amore, English horn, clarinet in D, clarinet in A, two clarinets in B flat, bass clarinet, four saxophones, four bassoons, double bassoon, eight horns, four trumpets, three trombones, bass tuba, four timpani, triangle, tambourine, glockenspiel, cymbals, bass drum and two harps, turned, after *Der Rosenkavalier,* to more modest ensembles, and achieved, in *Ariadne auf Naxos,* something that critics to this day see fit to call Mozartean.

It is difficult even now to determine how far this reaction was prompted by sincere revulsion against a type of music based so obviously on the excessive and how far by a common recognition that one could go no further within the framework of what convention accepted as serious or classical music. Doubtless it was a little of both. The voluminous critical writings of the composers involved indicate that the impulse and desire to return to a more musical music was sincere. But recognition of a technical impasse is common to them all.

From an esthetic point of view they all perceived that music had strayed far from the musical track, that it had, indeed, got on to a siding without an outlet, and that the thoughtless consumption of harmonic and orchestral resources had led to a kind of physical growth best described in terms of obesity and elephantiasis, to a mental and spiritual growth suggestive of megalomania, delusions of grandeur, hallucination, and senility.

It is significant that in their discussions of the various aspects of technical exhaustion, the composers deal almost exclusively with the problem of harmony. There is little talk of the orchestra or of instrumentation. This is doubtless attributable in great measure to the fact that the neo-classical point of view has again focused attention on the classical criteria of melodic and harmonic rather than orchestral construction, and has produced a type of music in which orchestration is no longer a primary element of structure and articulation.

It is also due, undoubtedly, to the basically correct conclusion that the central crisis of Western music is the exhaustion of harmonic resources. The orchestra is not really exhausted. That it has remained relatively stagnant for fifty years is due to the fact that composers have not been able to progress harmonically.

It is here that the juxtaposition of contemporary serious and contemporary popular music offers a clue to the riddle of contemporary musical evolution. Whereas the serious composer has taken orchestration for granted and devoted himself to problems of harmony and form, the popular composer has taken harmony for granted and continued with the development of the orchestra.

No one will question the extent to which the various types of jazz orchestra are derived from the symphony orchestra. In the best hot jazz the connection between the jazz ensemble and the symphony orchestra may be hard to discern, but in the many intermediate types of commercial jazz, particularly the "sweeter" varieties, the kinship and derivation are unmistakable. What the good "sweet" arrangements owe to Strauss, Debussy, Ravel and even the early Stravinsky must be obvious to anyone with ears to hear and the experience to make comparisons and draw conclusions.

In other words, jazz represents an instinctive popular recognition of the fact that it was only the composers, not the public, who had reached a limit with the orchestral extravaganzas of the last decade before the First World War, and that it was the composers, not the public, who had had enough. Jazz has gone far beyond the symphony orchestra of 1912. The band is not so big, for jazz is geared fast to economics, but it can be and often is louder, richer, and more exciting. One might even describe it as a refinement of the sound of the symphony orchestra, but without the fury.

Unfettered by tradition, and unencumbered by excess instruments and intellectual baggage, it can react immediately to the fluctuations of popular taste. It has developed some instruments of its own, particularly the saxophones, and has made over in its own image such traditional instruments as the trumpet, the trombone, and the clarinet. Except in the very "sweet" bands it has discarded the string quartet, which is not strong enough for such vivid company. And it has brought the double-bass player up to date, simply and wisely, by taking away his bow.

In one sense, the evolution of the orchestra from Strauss and Ravel to the top commercial bands is as logical as anything that has happened in music in the twentieth century. If the ultimate creative phase of European music was the orchestral phase, then it stands to reason that the orchestra, as the youngest of music's resources, was also the least exhausted. In continuing the evolution of the orchestra, popular music has simply reacted to a trend of popular taste that European music had already discovered and made apparent.

Not that jazz is pure orchestration. Much of it certainly is, at least to the extent of determining the superiority of one band or arranger over another. But the fundamentals are the eternal ones of melody and rhythm. How melody and rhythm are presented is always a matter of contemporary taste, habit, and convention. The twentieth century has not lost its love for instrumental novelty, brilliance, richness, and virtuosity. This is something that the makers of jazz have never forgotten or ignored. Nor could they afford to. They work at it for a living, and they work within the terms of the culture and economy of their time, as the great composers always have worked.

The composers of modern music, on the other hand, faced with the exhaustion of traditional materials, but bound to a tradition that cannot live without precisely these materials, have had no choice but to go back. Even the orchestra, which was far from exhausted, was ruled out for them as an area for further exploration, since they were committed to using it within the traditional harmonic framework of European music.

The orchestra—the great unexhausted resource—and the initiative in musical evolution thus passed to popular music by default.

THE CRISIS OF OPERA

✦ ✦
✦

THE harmonic epoch of European music was born in the opera house.

Although its evolution has been dominated by the trend from an originally vocal art to an ultimately instrumental art, opera has remained one of its great representative forms. All the evolutionary factors in European music have been present in the evolution of opera, and many of them originated in opera.

It would be impossible, of course, to write a complete history of European music with reference to opera alone, but any satisfactory history of opera will cover all the evolutionary factors essential to a critical understanding of European music. A critical coverage of Monteverdi, Alessandro Scarlatti, Handel, Gluck, Mozart, Cimarosa, Beethoven, Rossini, Meyerbeer, Weber, Donizetti, Bellini, Verdi, Gounod, Massenet, Wagner, Mascagni, Puccini, Strauss, Debussy, and Berg would provide all that is needed to describe the arc of the rise and fall of European music.

The decisive factors throughout the story are harmony and the orchestra. That it is impossible to list the singer among these factors gives to the story the flavor of perversity that so distinguishes the history of European music. This history offers, in its boldest outlines, the spectacle of an instrumental art born of a vocal art, which made a singer of the orchestra, and collapsed when the vocal objective was forgotten.

The singer himself has remained without influence. At each step along the way he has had to yield to the overriding demands of the orchestra. He has had his moments, to be sure. There were times in both the eighteenth and nineteenth centuries when the singer ruled the roost, and composers did his bidding. But the trend of musical evolution was against him. History records these as bad periods. They were terminated by reform movements born of the conviction that there was more to music than mere singers could provide.

This "more" was always found in harmony and in the orchestra. The implications of harmony seemed more substantial than the blandishments of a tune, however meltingly or forcefully delivered, and the instrument of harmony was the orchestra. Thus it is that the three-century history of opera shows the singer in a long battle with the orchestra, a battle punctuated by dramatic fluctuations, but with the outcome never in doubt.

The tragedy is that the nature of the conflict and its implications were not understood, even by the contestants. The reform composers, notably Gluck, Wagner, and Verdi, never fully realized that in favoring the orchestra they were imposing upon it vocal responsibilities. And the singers who acquiesced in the surrender of their primacy, themselves fascinated by the orchestra and the challenge of orchestra participation, failed to realize that what they were losing was their life's blood of vocal melody.

Nor were the implications of the conflict apparent to the public. They are not understood to this day. The opera-going public, to be sure, still favors *The Barber of Seville, Lucia, Norma, Il Trovatore, Tannhäuser,* and *La Bohème,* all singers' operas. But few are disposed to challenge the historical judgment of *Otello* or *Falstaff* as Verdi's masterpieces, or of *Tristan und Isolde* as Wagner's. One simply deplores the unenlightened condition of public taste. The public accepts the disparagement—and continues to pay allegiance to its favorites.

Thus it is that the low estate of contemporary opera, while recognized, is not understood as a consequence of evolutionary forces still enthusiastically applauded. History goes no further than noting that, up to the time of *Der Rosenkavalier*, opera was a living art and that since then it has not been. There is little disposition to seek in Wagner, Verdi, and Strauss the root of the evil.

Characteristic of modern opera generally are the assignment of the musical expressive function to the orchestra and the reduction of the singer to the role of a recitative-articulating actor. The idiom of the orchestra, in turn, is what is familiar to all of us as modern music. In this respect the iniquities of modern opera are identical with the iniquities of modern music in general, with the single exception that opera is better suited than other forms to deriving some benefit from the descriptive faculties that came to the fore in the decadence of the art.

The contemporary idiom of the singer is the parlando recitative, inherited from the last great manifestations of Italian opera, and the declamatory style inherited from Wagner. Gone are the arias, duets, trios, quartets, quintets, sextets, septets, and grand choruses that so delighted the audiences of Mozart, Beethoven, Weber, Rossini, Donizetti, Bellini, Verdi, Puccini—and even of Wagner and Strauss.

All successful operas have succeeded because they have given musical pleasure and excitement, because the audience's attention has been held and its spirit moved by beautiful singing, stirring drama, a great spectacle or—as is the case with the most successful operas—by the three in combination. No opera has succeeded that did not give singers something to sing. At its best, opera is the extension of the theater in song, the expressive faculties of vocal melody being exploited to broaden and intensify the emotional communication.

Opera owes its existence as an art of the theater to the dramatic implications of harmony. This is why opera, like the symphony and the symphonic poem, exists only in European music. Harmony is articulate, however, only in song, whether the singing be entrusted to voices or to instruments. In opera the singing was originally entrusted to singers, since the purpose was the representation of drama, and the technique the articulation of drama by singing actors. But as the orchestra emerged as the ideal instrument of harmonic music, the singer had to adjust himself to a concept of music that recognized the orchestra as the dominant executive agent.

Modern opera is the result of interpreting this as a trend directed, not only against the singer, but also against song. Overlooked is the fact that in *Tristan und Isolde* and *Otello* the orchestra sings. Wagner and Verdi sensed instinctively that there can be no music without song. When they inhibited the singing of their singers by grafting the vocal line to the text, they saw to it that the melodic loss was made good in the orchestra. Their successors simply noted the absence of set vocal pieces and concluded that Wagner and Verdi had evolved something better than song.

Thus it is that for fifty years composers have given us recitative and parlando operas that disdain the agreeable sensuous communication of song, vocal or instrumental, without substituting for it the precise articulation of the spoken word. They have given us operas which, uncommunicative musically, are dependent for communication upon the text. The singer is restricted to declamation in order that the text may be understood. And then he is drowned out by a clamorous orchestra in order that the composer may still claim to have written an opera.

The contemporary composer makes a point of integrating music and drama, and achieves neither one nor the other— nor anything else. If one listens to the music, the experience is unrewarding, since, as the composer will be the first to proclaim, it is unintelligible without reference to the drama. But if one listens to the drama, nothing comes of it but frustration, since the text is normally lost in the orchestral din.

The villain of the piece, of course, is Wagner. Modern opera, like all modern music, is reactionary, and no other composer is so stigmatized by the reaction as Wagner. The length of his operas, his system of leit-motifs, the size and richness of his orchestra, the fullness of his harmonies, the ecstasies of his progressions, the philosophical pretentions of his libretti—all are rejected. But these have to do with manner rather than with method. Wagner's method—the integration of music and drama, with music subordinate to the text —has survived. The irony of this is that no composer has ever so flagrantly and successfully violated his own proclaimed method. Wagner's music has survived, not because of his method, but in spite of it.

The simple fact is that people go to the Wagnerian music-dramas to hear the music—in the orchestra and on the stage. They go to hear *The Ride of the Valkyries*, the *Waldweben*, *Wotan's Farewell*, the *Magic Fire Music*, *Winterstürme*, *Du bist der Lenz*, Siegfried's *Funeral March* and *Rhine Journey*, Brünnhilde's *Immolation, O sink hernieder Nacht der Liebe*, the *Liebestod*, and so on—all musical episodes of lyric, epic, and sometimes even dramatic grandeur.

Hardly anyone understands the words. Hardly anyone cares, except possibly the singers, for whom they serve as memory props and a guide to expressive vocal coloration. The audience is required to sit a long time between these musical pleasures. It puts up with a good deal of awful boredom during those barren stretches where Wagner really practiced what he preached. A good many people consider it worth the trouble, and some are even impressionable enough to persuade themselves that they enjoy the ugly, empty wastes of Wagnerian recitative.

The purely musical basis of Wagner's popularity is something contemporary composers of opera have never perceived. They have held to his method and discarded his manner, not recognizing that what was valid and vital in Wagner was precisely his manner, including particularly the excesses and extravagances the contemporary composer so heartily despises.

Wagner was a musician, a composer in spite of himself. He achieved success and immortality in the theater just as Bellini and Meyerbeer and Verdi did—by writing hit tunes. He was music's greatest unwitting hypocrite. He was determined to bridle the singer. But instinctively he realized the telling effect of a well-prepared, forcefully delivered high C as the climax of a long melodic line. And Wagnerian opera today is dominated by the tenor and the prima donna just as any other opera is; indeed, even more so, since so few singers can meet their requirements.

Wagner compounded the paradox by adding a new virtuoso—the conductor. In his music, for the first time, orchestra and singer are on an equal footing. When the singer does not sing, the orchestra does. Often they sing together. For the orchestra's song the conductor is responsible. Since Wagner's time, with the primacy of the orchestra established, the conductor has been to opera what the castrato was to the opera of the seventeenth and eighteenth centuries.

It would probably have been impossible to continue much farther in the Wagnerian direction—that is, in the direction pointed by Wagner's musical manner. There had to be a limit to loudness and richness and bigness. Wagner did not reach it. But he came close, and Strauss had no difficulty in finishing the job with *Salomé*, *Elektra*, and *Der Rosenkavalier*.

The contemporary composer's error has been, not in failing to take up where Wagner and Strauss left off, but in failing to understand what Wagner had been. They were influenced by his theories and his method, and ignored the obvious musical reasons for his success. They neglected to note that the essential musical nature of opera had not been changed, least of all by Wagner, and that in the opera house, as in the concert hall, vocal melody, or an instrumental substitute for it, is the alpha and omega of music.

This is an axiom Verdi never overlooked, even in theory. It has made him, for the contemporary composer, a more complicated point of departure.

Despite the great successes scored by singers in Wagner's music-dramas, the impact of Wagner's personality, the novelty of his idiom, and the evangelistic fervor of its propagation blinded even the sophisticated to the essentially melodic source of his popularity. Hanslick, for instance, for all his insight, kept attacking the Wagnerian method as if it were the method that really counted.

Verdi's course from *Nabucco* to *Falstaff* was more gradual, and was accomplished without the fanfare of theoretical revelation and the dogma of a reform platform. But Verdi could not entirely escape the trend of the time. He never lost sight of the singer, but he did, toward the end, begin to lose sight of song. Hanslick felt this when he heard *Otello* in Milan in 1887, shortly after the premiere, and commented:

"Song remains the decisive element, but it follows closely the course of thought, feeling, and word. Independent, self-sufficient, symmetrically constructed melodies appear less frequently than does that cross between recitative and cantilena which now dominates modern opera. . . . If the right choice of color for every mood and the emphatic notation of every turn of speech were the single objective of opera, then we could unhesitatingly declare *Otello* to be an improvement over *Aïda* and Verdi's finest work.

"This devotion to the poem does not, however, release the opera composer from other obligations. He must above all else be a musician, and on this basis we expect music not only in accord with the text but also attractive to us simply as music—individual, original, and self-sufficient. . . . We demand of the opera composer beauty and novelty of musical ideas, particularly melodic ideas. And from this point of view *Otello* strikes me as less adequate than *Aïda, La Traviata* or *Un ballo in maschera.*" [27]

To the succeeding generation it did not appear, as it did in the case of Wagner, that Verdi had reached a limit. They reckoned that his was a direction offering reasonable prospects of further profitable vistas. This proved to be the case, if in a limited degree. The job of running out the vein, performed for German opera by Strauss and for French opera by Debussy and Charpentier, was done for the Italians by Leoncavallo, Mascagni, Giordano, and Puccini. But again the composers committed a critical error, or, to put it more precisely, an error in criticism.

Their mistake was in thinking of the succession of Verdi's operas in general terms of continuous progress, from bad to good to better to best, the last applying to *Otello* and *Falstaff*. In terms of technical mastery and dramatic sophistication this was certainly the case. But it was not the case in terms of music. The composer, the student of music, the sophisticated listener, may think of *Otello* as being superior to *Aïda*, and of *Falstaff* as being superior to *Otello*. But as pure music *Aïda* is superior to both of them.

The composers turned to *Otello* and *Falstaff* to find out what it was that Verdi was driving at. They found something very much akin to the Wagnerian concept of integrated music-drama, free of Wagner's Germanic trappings. What they failed to understand was that even Verdi could be wrong, or at least go too far. Verdi's destination was *Aïda*. He had developed a considerable momentum in getting there, and in *Otello* and *Falstaff* he overshot the objective. He did not come to grief. He had too much stability for that. But his successors foundered in rapid succession.

It is easy to understand, at this distance, the temptation *Otello* and *Falstaff* represented. They offered more concentrated, more pointed, more modern excitement and pleasure. The pace is faster, the action more direct and, in the case of *Otello*, more violent and shocking. The form is less conventional. The set piece has almost vanished. There are some in *Otello*, although less numerous and less conspicuous than in *Aïda*. There are very few in *Falstaff*. In other words, they represented, when superficially examined, and from the point of view of the time, a liberation from the operatic conventions, a step toward real music-drama, a closer approximation than Wagner was able to achieve of a complete jelling of the various arts involved in opera.

Such an appreciation was correct enough, but the conclusions drawn from it were as mistaken as those drawn from the similar appreciation of Wagner, and hardly less disastrous, although easier to forgive. Verdi was the more honest progressive of the two, or at least the more consistent, and his results were more convincing. Wagner's visions were a bit ridiculous. Verdi's never were. He had as good a sense of the theater as Wagner, and a more conscious understanding of the essentially musical nature of opera. Thus it was easy to believe that *Otello* and *Falstaff* owed their success and the high esteem in which they were held to what was new in them rather than to what was old.

This was true as far as the critics and the initiated public were concerned. But it was not the new that kept the operas in the repertoire. It was what still survived of the earlier Verdi. Critics may praise as they will the declamatory style of *Otello*. But what keeps it in the repertoire is the opening chorus, the Drinking Song, the first act duet, the Credo, the Iago-Otello duet at the close of the second act, the great choral scene and Otello's monologue at the end of the third act, and Desdemona's arias in the fourth. There are fewer such melodic excursions in *Falstaff*, which is why *Falstaff* is less often in the repertoire than *Otello*.

Contemporary composers would have done better had they not dismissed the fact that *Aïda* is still more popular than either *Otello* or *Falstaff* and always will be. Their error was in listening to the critics rather than to the box-office. About this even Verdi, for whom the box-office was never an institution to be taken lightly, may have been deceived. By the time *Otello* was produced he had achieved a position in the hearts of his countrymen and others where failure would have been next to impossible. But the fact was that Verdi, along with the main stream of music, had moved away from his popular base. He, too, had been seduced by the lure of a music that would be more than song.

This is the tragedy of European music in miniature. In aspiring to more than song its composers denied those very lyric faculties of music which prompt people to express themselves musically and which make the musical expression of others intelligible. Preoccupied with harmony and instrumentation, they forgot that the musician's primary purpose in life is to sing.

European music collapsed, but not just because its distinctive technical resources were exhausted. It collapsed because composers thought of composition in terms of technique. They knew a lot about composition, but they no longer knew anything about music. They had forgotten, if they ever knew, what music is. Nowhere is this more convincingly demonstrated than in the history of opera.

The normal means of communication is speech. All speech is colored by variations of pitch and rhythm employed spontaneously to supplement the precision or imprecision of words with a sense of the feelings associated with them. Thus all speech is in some degree musical, and all speakers composers, in however rudimentary a way. Verbal communication is never entirely dissociated from musical communication. Musical expression begins when a baby first uses its vocal chords.

Poetry is a musical extension of speech. It is distinguished from speech by a rhythmical organization whose purpose is to encourage, support, and animate a vocal tone more consciously and more consistently sustained than is customary or practical in speech.

The advantage of the sustained tone of poetry over the unsustained tone of speech is its plasticity. The melodic variation can be enriched and accentuated, and the opportunities for expressive coloration are infinitely increased, if only because the tone is of longer duration and gives the speaker more time for its lyrical exploitation. Poetry is, in short, a step toward song. Although an understanding of the words is still essential to a satisfactory communication, the melodic component is on at least a level with the verbal.

If one wishes to go beyond the poet's capacities for sensuous, or melodic communication, song is the next step. Here the voice is fully sustained, and the melodic component of the communication dominant, if not exclusive. The words rather cease to count. The communication is sensuous rather than ideational, general rather than precise. The words are hardly more than a guide to the singer. They are not essential to the audience. This is why songs in all languages are effective everywhere, regardless of the language in which they are sung, provided only that they are good songs and well sung.

Song has the advantage over prose and poetry of an incomparably greater range of expressive coloration and emphasis, since the tone can be regulated in pitch, augmented or diminished in volume, and accelerated or retarded in movement in a purely musical way. Because of sustained plastic, malleable tone, music can work in expressive spheres where prose, bound to the word, and poetry, released from absolute verbal precision but still constrained by a text, cannot go. This is why the poet writes verse instead of prose, and it is why the musician should work with song rather than with verse.

The historical course of music since Beethoven's time has been in the opposite direction. Musicians have acted as though music's ideational imprecision were a fault, and as though its salvation lay in finding in it the narrative and descriptive faculties which are the natural attributes of speech, poetry, painting, and sculpture. This was because the picturesque and dramatic implications of harmony and orchestra led them to assume that music's ultimate objectives were dramatic and picturesque.

There have been similarly misguided ambitions in the sister arts. Prose writers have abandoned syntax and rhetoric in order to achieve something akin to poetry. Poets have abandoned the precision of word and meter in order to achieve something akin to music. Painters have abandoned description in order to achieve something akin to architecture. The overall picture is plainly pathological—a disheartening spectacle in which creative artists, secretly aware that they cannot match or surpass their predecessors, crib from their neighbors in order, at least, to be original.

In opera this general tendency has found expression in a denial of purely musical values in favor of textual or descriptive values. Instead of making opera the extension of the theater in song, composers since Wagner's and Verdi's time have tended to make it a theatrical extension of music. They have behaved as if song were something to be ashamed of—and have produced a songless music of which they should be ashamed.

Parlando recitative or dry declamation has replaced the aria and the concerted piece. Choral commentary has replaced the exuberant song of massed voices. Ballet has disappeared, by which opera has been deprived, not only of song, but of dance. Even the orchestra, opera's last great singer, has become an humble provider of commas, periods, exclamation points, descriptive color, inflated dynamic contrasts, and mood-painting. The faculties of free, emotional, sensuous expression in song, which are music's purest and most utterly native property, have been denied, as if composers were all ascetics, and song a cardinal sin.

Asceticism is one of the abiding ills of modern music. Asceticism and music do not go together. Music is a spontaneous, uninhibited expression of feeling. Without feeling there can be no music. Asceticism is opposed to the expression of feeling and the indulgence of the senses. This is why ascetic faiths and philosophies have no music and why, in certain austere faiths, music is associated with evil.

It is in the opera house that the ascetic character of modern music is most keenly felt. A symphony without song may deceive by its thematic workmanship and the skill and ingenuity of its orchestration. In the opera house, with attention diverted from the orchestra to the stage, the absence of song is insupportable. For there is less music in the declamation of modern opera than in the spoken lines of the modern theater.

The kind of declamation or parlando recitative now fashionable in modern opera defeats rather than assists the musical objective. By restricting the voice to arbitrary pitches in a manner incompatible with the melodic-structural character of song, the composer puts the singer in an emotional straightjacket. The vocal line to which he is constrained offers less opportunity for melodic expression than the flattest sort of speech.

Nothing has been written in the opera since the end of World War I that could compare as music with any Shakespearean speech, even as delivered by a third-rate actor. Thus it is that modern opera reveals the full calamity of serious music. An art that originated as the creative extension of the rudimentary music of speech has ended, in the more radical of its present forms, by being less musical than the gurgle of a newborn babe.

There is little, as usual, that the composer can do about it, even if he recognizes the fact. If he tries to write musically he ends, like Krenek twenty years ago, in a no-man's land between serious and popular music, or like Menotti today, somewhere between the present and Puccini. Or he finds, as did Weill, that he can compete successfully with the really popular composers, and does so. In either case he ceases to be taken seriously as a serious composer. If he continues in directions still taken seriously he may make a reputation, but he will hardly make money. Certainly he will not make music.

Music still lives in the theater. It probably always will. But it lives in the theater today, in America, at least, in the music of Gershwin, Kern, Rodgers, Porter, Schwartz, and Berlin. Their shows have never been fully recognized as opera. But it is not what a thing is called that counts. It is what it is. If opera is the extension of the theater in song, then these shows are operas, regardless of the spoken dialogue and regardless of who does the orchestration.

By the same definition most modern opera is not.

THE CRISIS OF EVOLUTION II

FROM the foregoing review of the contemporary composer's technical preoccupations, one conclusion seems obvious: he is looking for a technical solution to what is not essentially a technical problem.

The composer is confusing ends and means. Music proceeds, not from the techniques of composition, but from a social requirement for musical expression. Techniques of composition are the means by which this requirement is satisfied according to society's tastes. They are valid only insofar as they serve a social objective.

The significant musical fact of this century is not atonality, nor neo-classicism, nor neo-primitivism. These are techniques derived, not from a popular musical requirement, but from the inability of the composer to express himself musically. Their purpose is not to satisfy a musical impulse but to disguise the absence of one.

The only musical fact of real significance is the new music for which there is a demand.

It is odd that composers have not understood this, because the traditions they seek to perpetuate were all shaped in their own time by demand. And the composers know it. The same men who propagate the legend that contemporary music is never appreciated in its own time insist upon upbraiding contemporary audiences for not having the thirst for new music that audiences had in the time of Bach, Haydn, and Mozart.

This habit of criticizing audiences instead of music has made of the contemporary composer what he is today: a pathetic figure seeking to shape the music of his generation while all around him the music of his generation is spontaneously and irresistibly taking place.

For the past fifty years music has been experiencing the most profound and fundamental evolutionary upheaval since 1600. It is not the change from a tonal to an atonal language, of which Krenek speaks, nor the return to old models and old concepts represented by neo-classicism.

It is rather the change from a music based on theme and harmony to a music based on melody and rhythm. It has taken place, not in serious music, but in popular music. And it has taken place, not because some composer or group of composers decided it ought to take place, but because society willed that it should take place.

There is no question but that the condition of music in 1910 invited revolution. Nor is there any doubt that revolution occurred. What the historians and critics have yet to grasp is that there was not one revolution but two, and that the revolution in serious music was no more than an academic exercise without popular roots. It was a soap box oration with only a coterie of the faithful as an audience.

The mobs were preoccupied with other things, in this case with other music. They were dancing to the new rhythm of their time, and singing its tunes. This was a musical revolution incubated, not in Vienna or in Paris, but in New Orleans and Chicago.

Historians, critics, and composers have made the mistake of thinking of the main stream of musical evolution solely in terms of serious music, as if there were a serious music and a popular music instead of simply various qualities of music.

The error is indicated by the fact that there is both vulgar serious music and select popular music.

The significant evolutionary fact is that both select and vulgar jazz have an audience, while new serious music of the more vulgar type has little popular following, and select serious music has none.

The evolutionary status of serious music can best be understood by thinking of the nineteenth century epoch as a main stream flowing confidently through a luxuriant valley—into a swamp. Modern music may then be understood as the effort of an enfeebled current to escape stagnation.

Continuing the metaphor, jazz may be thought of as a current that bubbled forth from a spring in the slums of New Orleans to become the main stream of the twentieth century. In less than fifty years it has flooded the United States and most of the rest of the world.

To put it briefly, the most important phenomenon of musical evolution occurred: a style was born.

The composer of modern music contemplates this phenomenon with lofty dispassion. He condescends now and then to crib jazz elements for exploitation in his own esoteric adumbrations, seeking to draw from the jazz idiom some of the vitality and actuality so notably lacking in his own. But it seldom occurs to him to consider jazz of evolutionary significance in a more than contributory sense.

He regards it rather as a provocative folk material upon which he may draw for more significant creations of his own. Apparently safe behind the assumption of the co-existence of two kinds of music, serious and popular, and of the superiority of serious music to popular music, he acknowledges jazz's original virtues without feeling threatened by its popularity.

He finds further comfort in the differences between audiences. Because his own music is heard and sometimes applauded by audiences drawn by Beethoven, he flatters himself that Beethoven's audience is also his. Failing to perceive that audiences change as well as idioms, and that the jazz audience is just as surely the real public of his generation as jazz is its music, he flatters himself that his—and Beethoven's —audience is the superior of the two.

His argument that the evolution of art music has never before been determined by the masses overlooks the fact that there has never before been a mass audience.

The course of musical evolution in the nineteenth century was determined by the European bourgeois community that set the cultural tone of the time. Evolution today is determined by an audience, not of thousands or hundreds of thousands, but of hundreds of millions. And the cultural tone of the time is set by what hundreds of millions of people like.

Today's serious music audience flatters itself that in perpetuating the European musical tradition it improves the cultural tone of the time. Many of its members, particularly in the United States, are members for no other reason. Subscribing to symphony concerts and community recital series is widely regarded as evidence of the subscriber's good citizenship.

In the sense that this audience supports and encourages ideal performances of European musical masterpieces, the claim of a cultural contribution is justified. But it is a contribution to the nineteenth century in the form of a historical summing up rather than a contribution to the twentieth in the form of a twentieth century music. The occasional performance of a new composition cannot disguise the autumnal flavor of the spectacle.

There is, indeed, nothing about the serious music scene that suggests a beginning or even a continuity. The familiar chronologically arranged program, beginning with Bach and ending with Bartok, is the symbol of a period of summation, an exercise in the study of European music. As such it is likely to be a good one, for the standards of performance are higher than they have ever been. Otherwise the serious music audience's contribution to culture hardly goes beyond its significance as a demonstration that the culture of the nineteenth century drove its roots wide and deep and died hard.

In short, the composer overlooks sociology. He writes for an audience whose concern is with the past, and in an idiom unintelligible to any audience at all. While he has been wrestling with the problem of adapting exhausted resources to a dying tradition, musical history has flowed on around him, leaving him a curiously innocent intellectual pocket to expire at his leisure.

In his preoccupation with his self-styled sovereignty as a creator of serious music, the contemporary composer confuses style and manner, and overlooks the real sovereignty of style, derived from the popularity which guarantees its validity as a genuine music. He ignores the implications of the fact that he can draw as he will upon jazz without creating anything but a pastiche, while jazz can draw with impunity upon the classics, and even upon him, without sounding any the less like jazz.

A strong style, like a strong current, absorbs every inferior stream that crosses its path. The proof of strength lies in the fact of absorption. In music today the fact is manifest. Jazz can absorb any of the technical devices of modern music without seeming to imitate. Modern music can absorb none of the musical characteristics of jazz without immediately sounding like an imitation of jazz.

This is difficult for the composer, the historian and the critic to understand. For all of them evolution implies continuity, and in relating jazz to the evolution of Western music the continuity is not immediately apparent. Even to the musicologist the superficial contrasts are so vivid that they tend to blot out the more important fundamental similarities.

Foremost among these contrasts is the fact that jazz seems to deny, or at least to lack, certain of the characteristics that make European music seem superior to all other musical cultures—notably an inferred philosophical or otherwise reflective content and the capacity to be sustained in large and enduring forms.

Jazz does not lend itself to analysis in terms of meaning, and its dimensions have often appeared to be circumscribed by the conventional contours of a popular refrain. Traditionally, it has proved most effectively susceptible of extension in a variation form. Jazz treatment of most melodies, i.e., a statement of the melody followed by a sequence of so-called choruses, is, indeed, nothing more than the old form of theme and variations, the difference being that the variations are usually more or less improvisational.

Jazz has not, however, been identified with other traditional forms of serious music, such as the sonata, the symphony, the concerto, etc., except for such excursions into the serious music field as the *Rhapsody in Blue,* the *Concerto in F* and *Porgy and Bess,* none of which is really jazz.

Jazz has ignored the symphony orchestra, considered indispensable to the greater manifestations of serious music, and has developed an orchestra of its own, derived from its own instrumental purposes. It has its own type of musician and singer, among whom native and original musicality rates above cultivated musicianship. And it has its own distinctive musical terminology.

The elements of continuity, however, are equally conclusive. The musical materials are the same, although differently employed. The scales are the same, and the manner in which melodies are derived from the scales is the same, whatever superficial differences there may be in the actual character and mood of the melodies. The influence of the symphony orchestra on the jazz orchestra is obvious. Most of the instruments are common to both orchestras, although the jazz band uses fewer instruments and employs them, on the whole, more efficiently.

The same is true of vocal styles. A blues or a torch song is as much in the Western ballad tradition as a Schubert *Lied* or an Italian aria. The difference, both in composition and performance, is a difference of style. Jazz has its own style, pitched to the microphone and the expressive habits of the time. Essentially, *"Ah! mio cor"* has simply become "You're breakin' my heart!"

Of equal importance is the question of harmony. Jazz, as we have seen, solved the harmonic problem by refusing to regard it as a problem. It accepted harmony as it was, and used it in the older traditional way to enrich the melodic contour and accommodate the Western ear's requirement for multiple-voiced sound.

What the Western ear likes, in common with all other ears, is melody in the form of a memorable tune. But the Western ear is accustomed to hearing more than one pitch at a time, to tones in harmonic combination, and would probably find unrelieved unaccompanied solos monotonous. Jazz accommodates the habit accordingly, but without being diverted from its fundamental melodic and rhythmic purposes.

Modern jazz has, to be sure, taken a more serious and adventurous view of harmony, and not always to its advantage. The bop movement, beginning in the mid-forties, was in part a rebellion against the harmonic and melodic conventions shaped by jazz evolution through the swing period. It abandoned improvised variations of a given tune in favor of free melodic improvisation over the tune's chords, and then went on to change the chords, too, giving to the jazz improvisation a more sophisticated harmonic character than jazz had ever had before.

Be that as it may, whether one speaks of the rudimentary

harmonic scheme of traditional jazz, or the more sophisticated product of the later progressives, there is no denying
the origins of jazz harmony in the harmony of serious music
at the turn of the century. The harmonic character of jazz
would be unthinkable without Debussy and Ravel.

The basic substance of the jazz style, however, is melodic
improvisation. Here, if one looks back beyond the nineteenth
century, the position of jazz within the framework of Western musical evolution becomes clear enough. Even as late as
Beethoven, improvisation was fashionable among composers,
and was one of the standard features of their appearances as
soloists. Certainly many of their compositions should be
thought of as the written record of an improvisation, refined
by critical afterthought.

Improvisation in jazz is, to be sure, more of a communal
proposition. In this respect it resembles not so much the virtuoso improvisations of a Bach, a Buxtehude, a Mozart, a
Clementi, or a Beethoven as the eighteenth century concerto
grosso.

In a real jam session the alternation of solos, small solo
groups, and full band occur at the whim of the players. In an
arrangement it occurs according to a plan, inspired, likely as
not, by previous improvisation, and worked out with the men
who do the playing. If the concerto grosso did not originate
in precisely this manner, its character and purpose were the
same. As with the jam session, the players rather than
the composer or arranger were regarded as the heroes of the
piece, and the purpose was to give good players something
new and good to play.

In both cases, the arrangement and the concerto grosso, the
form derives from the normal desire of good musicians to
show their stuff in a style congenial and intelligible to their
listeners. It also derives from the normal desire of the real
musician to compose, or at least to invent and improvise and
embellish. The student of contemporary music is inclined to

forget that the separation of composer and performer is of comparatively recent origin.

This is not to say that earlier composers wrote only in order to play. But the impulse to compose seems in most cases to have originated in the impulse to play. In the days when new music was popular and in demand, they wrote primarily, as Honegger has observed, in order to enrich their repertoire. This is precisely the case with most jazz composers today.

A similar parallel exists with respect to liberties. The serious musician who takes liberties with the score is considered an infidel. The jazz musician who does not is considered a dolt. This was true, generally, of European music as late as the first quarter of the nineteenth century. Most composition in the seventeenth and eighteenth centuries left a good deal to the performer's imagination and discretion.

Faced with the choice between the serious musician's solemn adherence to the score and the jazz musician's spontaneous invention, it is difficult not to opt for the latter. The serious musician, of course, has no choice. He works in a style where the composer is now sovereign, and the music he plays is supposed to be played either as written or as subsequently arranged. But there is no reason why the listener should not find the phenomenon wanting in fantasy once the composer's own fantasy has become a familiar text.

There is no denying that this reverence for the composer, this worship of the written composition, has stultified musical imagination and inhibited our present enjoyment of European music by a heavy amalgam of academicism and sanctimoniousness. It is only fair to add that much of the solemnity and ritual of the present-day concert hall would have struck at least the earlier composers of the music still played there as ridiculous.

It is possible to see the history of European music in the nineteenth century as a successful effort by composers to fight

free of the musical conventions of the preceding century and
to establish the composer as a creative authority superior to
the practicing musician.

In the same manner it is also possible to see the history of
American popular music in the twentieth century as a successful effort by practicing musicians to fight free of the obstacles to spontaneous musical invention represented by formal composition.

Those who think of modern music as the final chapter in
the long decadence of European music conveniently date the
downward curve from Beethoven. He established the composer as a poet and philosopher, and furrowed the brow of
both listener and performer. From his time dates the sanctity
of the composition, the introduction of reverence into the
concert hall and the opera house, and the promotion of the
performer to the role of an interpreter of the composer's reve-
lations.

But if one thinks of music in terms of spontaneous invention by practicing musicians, then it would seem more accurate to date decadence from the time when composers began
writing out the inner voices of their harmonies, composing
accompaniments and embellishments, and restricting solo improvisation to cadenzas signaled by a six-four chord whose
purpose was to announce to the audience that from here on
the soloist was on his own.

From this point of view the great evolutionary accomplishment of jazz appears to be the elimination of the composer.
Just how far serious music stands from this course of evolution can be seen in the fact that while jazz is removing the
composer as an obstacle between musician and audience, the
composer of modern music seeks to remove the musician as
an obstacle between his own inspiration and his listener.

There is no absolute elimination, of course, of either composer or practicing musician. In jazz there is a germinal idea,

a basic melody, which somebody has to invent; and serious music, if it is to be heard, has to be played. But in jazz the composer is flattered to have his original idea serve as a take-off point for the imaginative excursions of fellow practicing musicians, just as Vivaldi was doubtless flattered to be plagiarized and embellished by Bach. The contemporary composer of serious music, on the other hand, writes purposely in such a way as to reduce the performer's intellectual and inventive contribution to a minimum.

Thus the jazz accomplishment is simply defined. It has taken music away from the composers and given it back to musicians and their public. The simplicity sought by serious composers through intellectual and technical experimentation has been achieved by practicing musicians guided by popular taste. Because of popular guidance their product is culturally valid. Because of the absence of popular guidance, the accomplishment of the serious composers is not.

This is obviously something the serious composer cannot admit, even to himself. But the fascination good jazz has for him indicates a strain of social susceptibility seldom apparent in his own compositions. Not even a man so dedicated as the composer to the concept of the composer's absolute social autonomy can be entirely immune to the trends of his own time.

He is fated to go on writing sonatas, symphonies, and operas as long as society as a whole continues to believe that these old forms and the symphony orchestra have a monopoly on respectability and cultural superiority. And there we leave him, apparently unaware—if not notably blissfully—that jazz is modern music—and that nothing else is.

BIBLIOGRAPHY

Superior numbers in the text refer to sources listed beside corresponding numbers in bibliography.

1. Artur Honegger, *Je suis compositeur,* Editions du Conquistador, Paris, 1951
2. Paul Hindemith, *A Composer's World,* Harvard University Press, Cambridge, 1953
3. W. H. Hadow, *The Vienna Period, Oxford History of Music,* Vol. V, Clarendon Press, Oxford, 1904
4. Paul Henry Lang, *Music in Western Civilization,* W. W. Norton & Co., New York, 1941
5. Oswald Spengler, *The Decline of the West,* Alfred A. Knopf, New York, 1932
6. Henry T. Finck, *Chopin and Other Musical Essays,* Charles Scribner's Sons, New York, 1889
7. Aaron Copland, *Our New Music,* Whittlesey House, New York, 1941
8. Roger Sessions, *The Musical Experience,* Princeton University Press, Princeton, 1950
9. Aaron Copland, *Music and Imagination,* Harvard University Press, Cambridge, 1952
10. Karl Geiringer, *Haydn, A Creative Life in Music,* W. W. Norton & Co., New York, 1946
11. Constant Lambert, *Music-Ho,* Faber & Faber Ltd., London, 1934
12. Aaron Copland, in *New York Times* Sunday Magazine, December 21, 1952
13. Ernst Krenek, *Selbstdarstellung,* Atlantis-Verlag, Zürich, 1948
14. Henry F. Chorley, *Thirty Years' Musical Recollections,* edited by Ernest Newman, Alfred A. Knopf, New York, 1926
15. Hector Berlioz, *Memoirs,* edited by Ernest Newman, Alfred A. Knopf, New York, 1935
16. Ernest Newman, *Fact and Fiction about Wagner,* Alfred A. Knopf, New York, 1931

17. Nicolas Slonimsky, *Lexicon of Musical Invective*, Coleman-Ross, New York, 1953

18. Willi Reich, "Alban Berg, 'Wozzeck,'" in *Musik der Zeit*, Heft 6, Verlag Boosey & Hawkes, Bonn, 1954

19. *Grove's Dictionary of Music and Musicians*, Macmillan, New York, 1949

20. Emil Pirchan, *Henriette Sontag*, Frick Verlag, Vienna, 1946

21. Giaocchino Rossini, *Ausgewaehlte Briefe*, Paul Szolnay Verlag, Vienna, 1947

22. Francis Toye, *Giuseppe Verdi*, Alfred A. Knopf, New York, 1931

23. Wallace Brockway and Herbert Weinstock, *Men of Music*, Simon and Schuster, New York, 1939

24. Casimir Wierzynski, *The Life and Death of Chopin*, Simon and Schuster, New York, 1949

25. Ernest Newman, *The Life of Richard Wagner (1813–1848)*, Alfred A. Knopf, New York, 1932

26. Eduard Hanslick, *Vienna's Golden Years of Music*, translated and edited by Henry Pleasants, Simon and Schuster, New York, 1950

27. Hans von Buelow, *Briefe*, Breitkopf & Haertel, Leipzig, 1908

28. S. Kracauer, *Orpheus in Paris*, Alfred A. Knopf, New York, 1938

29. *International Cyclopedia of Music and Musicians*, Dodd, Mead & Co., New York, 1946

30. Giuseppe Adami, *Puccini Briefe*, Werk Verlag, Berlin, 1944

31. Igor Stravinsky, *Poetics of Music*, Harvard University Press, Cambridge, 1947

32. Theodore Stravinsky, *Le message d'Igor Strawinsky*, Verlag Librairie F. Rouge, S.A., Lausanne, 1948

33. Ernst Krenek, *Studies in Counterpoint*, G. Schirmer, Inc., New York, 1940

34. Eric Walter White, *Stravinsky, A Critical Survey*, John Lehmann, London, 1947

35. Paul Hindemith, *Unterweisung im Tonsatz*, B. Schott's Soehne, Mainz, 1937

36. Fritz Rothschild, *The Lost Tradition in Music*, Oxford University Press, New York, 1953

37. Ralph Kirkpatrick, *Domenico Scarlatti*, Princeton University Press, Princeton, 1953

ABOUT THE AUTHOR

Henry Pleasants began his career as a music critic as a specialist in contemporary music. Following studies in voice, piano and composition at the Philadelphia Conservatory and the Curtis Institute of Music, he joined the Philadelphia *Evening Bulletin* in 1930 as assistant music critic. Arthur Tubbs, the paper's veteran theater and music editor, cared little for modern music. The result was that Mr. Pleasants, as a neophyte second-string critic, got the first-string assignments if modern music were involved. Thus he covered such important premiers in the early thirties as the Philadelphia Ochestra productions of *Wozzeck*, Stravinsky's *Oedipus Rex*, Prokofiev's *Pas d'Acier*, Chavez's ballet *H.P.*, Louis Gruenberg's *The Emperor Jones*, etc., along with the host of new and experimental orchestral compositions with which Leopold Stokowski was making a name for himself as a champion of modern music at that time.

In 1935, at the age of twenty-five, Mr. Pleasants succeeded Tubbs as Musical Editor of the *Evening Bulletin*, and continued in that post until entering the Army in 1942. In addition to his work for the *Bulletin*, he was a regular contributor to *Modern Music* and was an occasional musical correspondent for both *The New York Times* and the *New York Herald Tribune*. In 1940 he collaborated with Tibor Serly on the first definitive article on Bela Bartok to appear in the United States. It was published in the April issue of *Modern Music*.

Since the war Mr. Pleasants has remained in Europe, first

with the Army and subsequently with the Foreign Service, without, however, abandoning his concern with music. He was for many years Central European music correspondent for *The New York Times.* More recently he has been a frequent contributor to *High Fidelity, HiFi Stereo Review* and *Jazz Quarterly.* He is married to Virginia Pleasants, the harpsichordist.

REPRESENTATIVE SIMON AND SCHUSTER PAPERBACKS

For people who want to know more about science, philosophy, the arts, and history in the making

Adler: *How to Read a Book*, $1.75
Ames: *What Shall We Name the Baby?*, $1.45
Bell: *Men of Mathematics*, $2.25
Berenson: *Rumor and Reflection*, $1.95
Berne: *A Layman's Guide to Psychiatry and Psychoanalysis*, $1.95
Brockway & Weinstock: *Men of Music*, $1.95
Burroughs: *Vasari's Lives of the Artists*, $1.95
Chayefsky: *Television Plays*, $1.75
Chernev & Harkness: *An Invitation to Chess*, $1.45
Cooke: *Playing the Piano for Pleasure*, $1.45
Dreyfuss: *Designing for People*, $1.95
Durant:
  The Pleasures of Philosophy, $1.75
  The Story of Philosophy, $1.75
Egri: *The Art of Dramatic Writing*, $1.75
Einstein & Infeld: *The Evolution of Physics*, $1.45
Fadiman:
  Fantasia Mathematica, $1.45
  Reading I've Liked, $2.25
Fellner: *Opera Themes and Plots*, $1.95
Fink: *Release from Nervous Tension*, $1.45
Ginzberg: *The Legends of the Jews*, $2.45
Gleaves & Wertenbaker: *You and the Armed Services*, $1.25
Goren:
  Contract Bridge for Beginners, $1.00
  Point Count Bidding, $1.00
Harriman: *Peace with Russia?*, $1.00
Heilbroner: *The Worldly Philosophers*, $1.50
Herment: *The Pipe*, $1.25
Horowitz: *Chess for Beginners*, $1.75
Horowitz & Reinfeld: *Chess Traps, Pitfalls and Swindles*, $1.45
Kazantzakis:
  Freedom or Death, $1.75
  The Greek Passion, $1.95
  The Odyssey, $2.95
  Zorba the Greek, $1.75
Kerr: *How Not to Write a Play*, $1.45
Laurence: *Men and Atoms*, $1.45
Lerner: *America as a Civilization*—VOL. 1, *The Basic Frame;* VOL. 2, *Culture and Personality,* each $1.95
Lovejoy: *Lovejoy's College Guide*, $3.50
Madrigal: *An Invitation to Spanish*, $1.25
Madrigal & Launay: *An Invitation to French*, $1.25
Mills: *The Causes of World War Three*, $1.50

Newman:
  What Is Science?, $1.95
  The World of Mathematics series
  Vol. 1, *Men and Numbers*, $2.95
  Vol. 2, *The World of Law and the World of Chance*, $2.75
  Vol. 3, *The Mathematical Way of Thinking*, $2.45
  Vol. 4, *Machines, Music and Puzzles*, $2.25
Oppenheimer: *The Open Mind*, $1.00
Pearson & Anderson: *U.S.A.—Second-Class Power?*, $1.75
Perelman:
  The Most of S. J. Perelman, $2.45
  The Road to Miltown, $1.45
Pirandello: *Short Stories*, $1.75
Platt: *The River of Life*, $1.75
Pleasants: *The Agony of Modern Music*, $1.45
Rosten: *A Guide to the Religions of America*, $1.50
Russell:
  Common Sense and Nuclear Warfare, $1.00
  A History of Western Philosophy, $2.75
  Human Knowledge, Its Scope and Limits, $2.25
  Unpopular Essays, $1.00
  Why I Am Not a Christian, $1.45
Schuster: *A Treasury of the World's Great Letters*, $2.25
Schwed: *Where Are the Customers' Yachts?*, $1.45
SCIENTIFIC AMERICAN BOOKS:
  Atomic Power, $1.45
  Automatic Control, $1.45
  Lives in Science, $1.45
  The New Astronomy, $1.45
  New Chemistry, $1.45
  The Physics and Chemistry of Life, $1.45
  The Planet Earth, $1.45
  Plant Life, $1.45
  The Scientific American Reader, $2.25
  Twentieth-Century Bestiary, $1.45
  The Universe, $1.45
Seldes: *The Public Arts*, $1.50
Shanet: *Learn to Read Music*, $1.45
Snyder & Morris: *A Treasury of the World's Great Reporting*, $2.75
Szilard: *The Voice of the Dolphins*, $1.00
Thurber: *Thurber Country*, $1.45
Turnbull: *The Great Mathematicians*, $1.25
Untermeyer: *Makers of the Modern World*, $2.95
Weinberg: *Attorney for the Damned*, $2.25
Wormser: *The Story of Law*, $2.95